Made in United States
Orlando, FL
07 August 2023

35823942R00072

ב"ה

My Siddur

הַסִדוּר שֶׁלִי

Nusach Ari - Chabad

Selected Prayers for Weekdays

Hebrew with English Transliteration
Ashkenazic/American Style Pronunciation

This Siddur belongs to

_____

This edition of My Siddur is not a complete Siddur.
It is a training tool to learn to pray in Hebrew.

My Siddur / HaSiddur Sheli 3.01 [Weekday]

Nusach Ari - Chabad, Hebrew with English Transliteration
Ashkenazic / American Style Pronunciation

First Edition, Chai Elul 5768, September, 2008
Second Edition, Chai Elul 5773, August, 2013
Third Edition, 3 Tamuz, 5774, June, 2014

TOOLS *for* TORAH
Revolutionizing Jewish Education

Proceeds from the sales of this book will enable more
Tools for Torah to be created and published.

This Siddur contains the holy Name of Hashem;
please treat it with the proper respect.

To the Rebbe
Rabbi Menachem M. Schneerson
who inspires us
to live meaningful lives
transforming our world into a place
where Hashem feels at home.

In Appreciation
of the Chabad Shluchim, Shluchos and their families
who tirelessly inspire and brighten the future
with the Rebbe's vision.

May they grow
from strength to strength
bringing nachat to Hashem
the Rebbe and all of Israel.

We Want Moshiach Now!

My Siddur – Customized!

Personalize the cover and a dedication page of My Siddur
for your personal/communal simchas, organizations, events, groups.

My Siddur's **Digitally Animated Edition**
and various Hard-Cover, Color Interior Editions
are available for full or partial sponsorship.

My Siddur is available (at the time of this printing) in these 4 editions*:
1. Weekday [This edition]
2. Weekday, Holiday, Bentching**
3. Shabbos, Holiday, Bentching
4. Weekday, Shabbos, Holiday, Bentching***

*All the Siddurim are Nusach Ari / Chabad and available in Sephard / Israeli style (Shabbat)
and Ashkenaz / American style (Shabbos) transliterations.
**Also includes Shabbos Kiddush & Torah / Haftarah Blessings.
***The common weekday prayers are not duplicated for Shabbos so there's lots of "flipping pages"
during the Shabbos prayers. Not recommended for regular Shabbos davening.

New Siddurim *in progress*:
5. My Siddur Translated, with non-literal, child-friendly translation. No transliteration.
6. My Siddur Hebrew Only. Without translations or transliterations. Just clear, large type.
7. Transliterated Bentcher with customizable cover for your simcha.
8. Translated Bentcher with customizable cover for your simcha.

See more and order on
www.ToolsforTorah.com

May all our prayers
pierce the heavens and reach G-d's throne,
swiftly returning with a positive response!

B"H

"*Sulam mutzav artza, v'rosho magia hashamaima – zohi tefila.*"
A ladder set on the ground, whose tip reaches the heavens - this is prayer. – The Zohar

The word "*tefila*" shares its root with "*tofel*" meaning "to attach."
Through *tefila* we attach, connect and bind ourselves to Hashem, our Creator. – Chassidic Teaching

My Siddur is designed to help climb the ladder of *tefila* in its original Hebrew, while focusing on the personal meaning and relevance of our prayers.

My Siddur features:

- **Large Hebrew text** for easy reading.
- **English Transliteration, divided by syl·la·bles** for accurate reading.
- **Mini Meditations** to help focus on the main theme of the *tefila*.
- **Bolded, Translated Keywords** in each *tefila*, for a glance during prayer and for guided discussion.
- **Starred Shva Na** for accurate Hebrew pronunciation.
- **Labeled Audio Trax** to hear and practice the correct pronunciation of each *tefila* (online or CD).
- **Prayers divided into short phrases, each on its own line,** for easy reading and comprehension.
- **Line Numbers** for tracking in class or group settings.

There are two versions of this *Nusach Ari - Chabad Siddur*, differing only in the pronunciation style of the transliteration, Sephardic and Ashkenazic (i.e. "Shabbat" vs. "Shabbos").

This Siddur has the *Ashkenazic (American) style* pronunciation.

About the Transliteration

My Siddur features words spelled out exactly as they sound (in the USA) to minimize confusing rules.

You may notice words transliterated differently than their common pronunciation. We did our best to transliterate the words accurately. (See "Transliteration Tips" on page ו.)

While the Siddur text transliteration is accurate, the table of contents, titles and instructions are written with the more commonly used transliterations.

Transliteration Tips:

1. Every *shva na* is honored with a "'" as in "ki·d'sho·nu."
2. The "ch" is pronounced as in the word "Challah."

Acknowledgements

With deep gratitude to G-d Almighty for enableing me to assist others on their spiritual journey, special thanks also goes to some who played a major role in the production of My Siddur;

Mrs. Rivkie Block for the original Siddur and Tefila Trax CD companion idea.

Rabbi Yosef B. Friedman of Merkos L'Inyonei Chinuch for granting permission to use the text of Siddur Tehilat Hashem in My Siddur.

Rabbi Yosef Hartmann for his ever ready, wise and practical assistance in all my publications, and Dr. Michael Abrahams for insights into the *tefilot*.

Chaya Mushka Braude for the majority of the brainstorming, transliterating, editing and formatting assistance. Chana (Eisenberg) Roberts, Rabbis Nochum Katsenelenbogen, Moshe Zaklikowski, Alex Heppenheimer and Shmuel Rabin for proofreading.

Rabbi Yossi Freedman (Argentina) for his invaluable direction, layout expertise and assistance.

Chava (Levin) Light for the magnificent cover art (ChavaStudios.com).

Rabbi Nissan Mindel OBM, whose books "My Prayer" volumes 1 & 2 (published by Kehot) inspired most of the Mini Meditations and explanations in My Siddur. (I urge anyone seriously interested in understanding and appreciating the concept of prayers in general and / or the specifics of each *tefila*, to read his priceless, beautifully written books.)

Rabbis Kugel, Ossey and Fried, the wonderful Shluchim of Chabad of the West Side, NYC, for their encouragement and support in "My Siddur" and other Tools for Torah publications. Our family is honored to be part of their team!

Mr. George Rohr and Rabbi Yossel Gutnick for their pioneering support of the first edition.

Most of all, my wife Sarah, for her incredible character and talent, thriving with all our family and work responsibilities while I am in "My Siddur" (and other publications') world, and also for the beautiful design of the Siddur pages and cover. To my children, Chana Mushka, Shayna Ruchama, Yehudis Bracha and Maryasha Esther for their continued enthusiasm and help.

Hashem loves to hear our prayers. Let us all pray that Hashem finally listen to His children's prayers and sends His righteous Moshiach, to take us all out of this *galut* (exile) and return us to the new, rebuilt Jerusalem where we will once again pray and serve Hashem in the *Beit Hamikdash* - the Holy Temple. May it happen now!

Rabbi Chayim B. Alevsky
3 Tamuz, 5774, July, 2014,
New York

How do I use *My Siddur*?

MINI MEDITATIONS... ...are these purple boxes above the *tefila*.
They help you medidate on the theme of the prayer.

KEYWORDS are the **bolded** words in the *tefila* text which appear with their loose translations at the bottom of the page. They provide an "at a glance" clue about the meaning of the *tefila*.

l'fa·ne·cha   a·ni   mo·deh
מוֹדֶה אֲנִי לְפָנֶיךָ, 1

מוֹדֶה
thanks

 Sit, stand, bow?

These little figures guide us in the position we should be during each *tefila*.

Music/Audio: You can pray, chant and sing along with our five professionally recorded, clearly articulated companion CDs. *Tefilot* are labled with their CD track #.

Notice the five styles of audio symbols, for each of the **five Trax series** for *My Siddur*:

Tefila II, Bentching II, Kabalat Shabbat, Shabbat Day and Holiday.*

SEE A CD LIST AND LEARN ABOUT HOW THE AUDIO CDs WORK, IN THE BACK PAGES OF THIS SIDDUR.

CDs and mp3 downloads can be purchased on ToolsforTorah.com, iTunes or Amazon.

My Siddur & the Bentching are currently available as Apps in iTunes etc.
Search for "My Siddur" and "Birkon" to listen the tefilot as you read them.

The world's first animated "**Living Siddur**" is in the midst of bringing the letters to life. Partner with us and see more on ToolsforTorah.com.

*When a tefila already exists elsewhere in My Siddur, its referring symbol is shaded:

Hebrew Aleph Beis Mini Guide

Letters sound like the *beginning* of their name, when a vowel is applied.

A ָ (*komatz*) under an א: "אָ" is "uh."   A ָ under a בּ: "בָּ" is "buh," etc.

Sound	Letter	Sound	Letter	Sound	Letter
P	פּ pay	K	כ kof	Sounds like its vowel	א aleph
F	פ fay	CH (kh) (Challah)	כ chof	B	בּ beis
F	ף final fay	CH (kh)	ך final chof	V	ב veis
TS	צ tzadik	L	ל lamed	G (hard)	ג gimel
TS	ץ final tzadik	M	מ mem	D	ד dalet
K	ק koof	M	ם final mem	H	ה hay
R	ר raysh	N	נ noon	V	ו vov
SH	שׁ shin	N	ן final noon	Z	ז zayin
S	שׂ sin	S	ס samech	CH (Challah)	ח ches
T	תּ tov	Sounds like its vowel	ע ayin	T	ט tes
S	ת sov			Y	י yood

Hebrew Vowels Guide

Vowels sound like the *beginning* of their name, when combined with a letter.

As in:	With א = Sounds	Vowel
up	uh = אָ	**ָ** K**u**hmatz
challah	ah = אַ	**ַ** P**a**tach
oy vay!	ay = אֵ	**ֵ** Tz**ay**reh
echo	eh = אֶ	**ֶ** S**e**gol
Israel	ih = אְ (Only has a sound when it begins the syllable, otherwise it's silent)	**ְ** Shi**h**va
oh yes!	oh = אֹ	**ֹ** Ch**o**lam
see	ee = אִ	**ִ** Ch**ee**reek
zoo	oo = אֻ	**ֻ** K**oo**bootz
zoo	oo = אוּ	**וּ** Sh**oo**rook
up	oh = אֳ	**ֳ** Chataf K**o**matz
challah	ah = אֲ	**ֲ** Chataf P**a**tach
echo	eh = אֱ	**ֱ** Chataf S**e**gol

Aleph Beis אַלֶף-בֵּית

ה ⁵ Hay	ד ⁴ Dalet	ג ³ Gimmel	ב Veis	בּ ² Beis	א ¹ Aleph

י ¹⁰ Yood	ט ⁹ Tes	ח ⁸ Ches	ז ⁷ Zayin	ו ⁶ Vov

ן Final Noon	נ ⁵⁰ Noon	ם Final Mem	מ ⁴⁰ Mem	ל ³⁰ Lamed	ך Final Chof	כ Chof	כּ ²⁰ Kof

ץ Final Tzadi(k)	צ ⁹⁰ Tzadi(k)	ף Final Fay	פ Fay	פּ ⁸⁰ Pay	ע ⁷⁰ Ayin	ס ⁶⁰ Samech

ת Sov	תּ ⁴⁰⁰ Tov	שׂ Sin	שׁ ³⁰⁰ Shin	ר ²⁰⁰ Reish	ק ¹⁰⁰ Koof

Vowels הַנְקֻדוֹת

וֹ Cholum חוֹלָם	ְ Shihva שְׁבָא	ֶ Sehgol סֶגוֹל	ֵ Tzayreh צֵירֵה	ַ Pahtach פַּתָּח	ָ Kuhmatz קָמַץ
ֱ Chataf Sehgol חֲטֶף סֶגוֹל	ֲ Chataf Pahtach חֲטֶף פַּתָּח	ֳ Chataf Kuhmatz חֲטֶף קָמַץ	וּ Shoorook שׁוּרֶק	ֻ Koobootz קֻבּוּץ	ִ Cheereek חִירִק

Practice Page

Kuhmatz קָמֵץ

אָ בָ גָ דָ הָ וָ זָ חָ טָ יָ כָ לָ מָ נָ סָ עָ פָ צָ קָ רָ שָׁ שָׂ תָ

Pahtach פַּתַח

אַ בַ גַ דַ הַ וַ זַ חַ טַ יַ כַ לַ מַ נַ סַ עַ פַּ צַ קַ רַ שַׁ שַׂ תַ

Tzayreh צֵירֶה

אֵ בֵ גֵ דֵ הֵ וֵ זֵ חֵ טֵ יֵ כֵ לֵ מֵ נֵ סֵ עֵ פֵ צֵ קֵ רֵ שֵׁ שֵׂ תֵ

Sehgol סֶגוֹל

אֶ בֶ גֶ דֶ הֶ וֶ זֶ חֶ טֶ יֶ כֶ לֶ מֶ נֶ סֶ עֶ פֶּ צֶ קֶ רֶ שֶׁ שֶׂ תֶ

Cheereek חִירִק

אִ בִ גִ דִ הִ וִ זִ חִ טִ יִ כִ לִ מִ נִ סִ עִ פִּ צִ קִ רִ שִׁ שִׂ תִ

Shihva שְׁוָא

אְ בְ גְ דְ הְ וְ זְ חְ טְ יְ כְ לְ מְ נְ סְ עְ פְּ צְ קְ רְ שְׁ שְׂ תְ

Koobootz קֻבּוּץ

אֻ בֻ גֻ דֻ הֻ וֻ זֻ חֻ טֻ יֻ כֻ לֻ מֻ נֻ סֻ עֻ פֻּ צֻ קֻ רֻ שֻׁ שֻׂ תֻ

Shoorook שׁוּרֻק

אוּ בּוּ בוּ גוּ דוּ הוּ וּ זוּ חוּ טוּ יוּ כּוּ כוּ לוּ מוּ נוּ סוּ עוּ פּוּ פוּ צוּ קוּ רוּ שׁוּ שׂוּ תּוּ תוּ

Cholum חוֹלُם

אֹ בֹּ בֹ גֹ דֹ הֹ וֹ זֹ חֹ טֹ יֹ כֹּ כֹ לֹ מֹ נֹ סֹ עֹ פֹּ פֹ צֹ קֹ רֹ שֹׁ שֹׂ תֹּ תֹ

Cholum חוֹלָם

אוֹ בּוֹ בוֹ גוֹ דוֹ הוֹ וֹ זוֹ חוֹ טוֹ יוֹ כּוֹ כוֹ לוֹ מוֹ נוֹ סוֹ עוֹ פּוֹ פוֹ צוֹ קוֹ רוֹ שׁוֹ שׂוֹ תּוֹ תוֹ

EVERYDAY/WEEKDAY PRAYERS

Read about the audio tracks and icons
in the back pages of this siddur.

MODEH ANI

Thank you, Hashem, for your kindness.
You returned my soul to me, refreshed.

Our very first words as we wake up in the morning. We are grateful and we show it!

l'fuh·neh·chuh   a·ni   mo·deh
1   מוֹדֶה אֲנִי לְפָנֶיךָ,

v'ka·yuhm   chai   Meh·lech
2   מֶלֶךְ חַי וְקַיָּם,

b'chem·luh   neesh·muh·si   bee   sheh·heh·che·zar·tuh
3   שֶׁהֶחֱזַרְתָּ בִּי נִשְׁמָתִי בְּחֶמְלָה,

eh·mu·nuh·seh·chuh   ra·buh
4   רַבָּה אֱמוּנָתֶךָ.

אֱמוּנָתֶךָ	נִשְׁמָתִי	מֶלֶךְ	מוֹדֶה
faith	soul	King	thanks

NETILAS YODAYIM

The Mitzvah to wash our hands,
to purify ourselves from the impurities of sleep.

We pour water from a large cup onto our hands (preferably at our bedside),
right - left, right - left, right - left.
After we take care of our bodily needs, we wash again the same way, at a sink
(in the kitchen or anywhere outside the restroom), and say:

huh·o·lum   Meh·lech   Elohaynu   Adonuy   Ah·tuh   Ba·ruch
5   בָּרוּךְ אַתָּה יְיָ, אֱלֹהֵינוּ, מֶלֶךְ הָעוֹלָם,

yuh·duh·yeem   n'ti·lahs   al   v'tzi·vuh·nu   b'meetz·vo·suv   ki·d'shuh·nu   ah·sher
6   אֲשֶׁר קִדְּשָׁנוּ בְּמִצְוֹתָיו, וְצִוָּנוּ עַל נְטִילַת יָדָיִם.

נְטִילַת יָדָיִם	בְּמִצְוֹתָיו	קִדְּשָׁנוּ
washing hands	with His commandments	He made us holy

ASHER YOTZAR

Thank you, Hashem for my health, allowing
my complex body to function properly.

(This *bracha* is also recited every time we use the restroom, after washing our hands.)

1 בָּרוּךְ אַתָּה יְיָ, אֱלֹהֵינוּ, מֶלֶךְ הָעוֹלָם,
Bo·ruch   Ah·tuh   Adonuy   Elohaynu   Meh·lech   huh·o·lum

2 אֲשֶׁר יָצַר אֶת הָאָדָם בְּחָכְמָה,
ah·sher   yuh·tzar   es   huh·uh·dum   b'chuch·muh

3 וּבָרָא בוֹ נְקָבִים נְקָבִים, חֲלוּלִים חֲלוּלִים,
u·vuh·ruh   vo   n'kuh·veem   n'kuh·veem   cha·lu·leem   cha·lu·leem

4 גָּלוּי וְיָדוּעַ לִפְנֵי כִסֵּא כְבוֹדֶךָ,
guh·looy   v'yuh·du·ah   leef·nay   chi·say   ch'vo·deh·chuh

5 שֶׁאִם יִסָּתֵם אֶחָד מֵהֶם,
sheh·eem   yi·suh·saym   eh·chud   may·hem

6 אוֹ אִם יִפָּתֵחַ אֶחָד מֵהֶם,
o   eem   yi·puh·say·ach   eh·chud   may·hem

7 אִי אֶפְשַׁר לְהִתְקַיֵּם אֲפִילוּ שָׁעָה אֶחָת.
ee   ef·shar   l'hees·ka·yaym   a·fee·lu   shuh·uh   eh·chus

8 בָּרוּךְ אַתָּה יְיָ, רוֹפֵא כָל בָּשָׂר, וּמַפְלִיא לַעֲשׂוֹת.
Bo·ruch   Ah·tuh   Adonuy   ro·fay   chuhl   buh·suhr   u·maf·li   la·ah·sohs

יָצַר	בְּחָכְמָה	רוֹפֵא	וּמַפְלִיא
formed	wisdom	Healer	does wonders

ELOKAI NESHAMA

Thank You for returning my pure,
holy neshama to me this morning.

Elohai
1 אֱלֹהַי,

hee   t'ho·ruh   bee   sheh·nuh·sa·tuh   n'shuh·muh
2 נְשָׁמָה   שֶׁנָּתַתָּ   בִּי   טְהוֹרָה   הִיא,

y'tzar·tuh   Ah·tuh   v'ruh·suh   Ah·tuh
3 אַתָּה   בְרָאתָהּ,   אַתָּה   יְצַרְתָּהּ,

b'keer·bee   m'sha·m'ruh   v'Ah·tuh   bee   n'fach·tuh   Ah·tuh
4 אַתָּה   נְפַחְתָּהּ   בִּי,   וְאַתָּה   מְשַׁמְּרָהּ   בְּקִרְבִּי,

mi·meh·ni   li·t'luh   uh·seed   v'Ah·tuh
5 וְאַתָּה   עָתִיד   לִטְּלָהּ   מִמֶּנִּי,

luh·vo   le·uh·seed   bee   ool·ha·cha·zi·ruh
6 וּלְהַחֲזִירָהּ   בִּי   לֶעָתִיד   לָבֹא.

b'keer·bee   sheh·ha·n'shuh·muh   z'mahn   kuhl
7 כָּל   זְמַן   שֶׁהַנְּשָׁמָה   בְּקִרְבִּי,

a·vo·sai   vAylohay   Elohai   Adonuy   l'fuh·ne·chuh   a·ni   mo·deh
8 מוֹדֶה   אֲנִי   לְפָנֶיךָ,   יְיָ   אֱלֹהַי   וֵאלֹהֵי   אֲבוֹתַי,

ha·n'shuh·mos   kuhl   A·dohn   ha·ma·ah·seem   kuhl   ri·bohn
9 רִבּוֹן   כָּל   הַמַּעֲשִׂים,   אֲדוֹן   כָּל   הַנְּשָׁמוֹת.

may·seem   leef·guh·reem   n'shuh·mos   ha·ma·cha·zeer   Adonuy   Ah·tuh   Bo·ruch
10 בָּרוּךְ   אַתָּה   יְיָ,   הַמַּחֲזִיר   נְשָׁמוֹת   לִפְגָרִים   מֵתִים.

מְשַׁמְּרָהּ	טְהוֹרָה	נְשָׁמָה
keep it	pure	soul

BIRCHOS HASHACHAR

Morning blessings of thanks.
Thank You Hashem for…

1

huh·o·lum   Meh·lech   Elohaynu   Adonuy   Ah·tuh   Bo·ruch
בָּרוּךְ אַתָּה יְיָ, אֱלֹהֵינוּ, מֶלֶךְ הָעוֹלָם...
Blessed are You Hashem our G-d, King of the Universe…

2

luy·luh   u·vayn   yohm   bain   l'hav·cheen   vi·nuh   la·sech·vi   ha·no·sayn
הַנּוֹתֵן לַשֶּׂכְוִי בִינָה, לְהַבְחִין בֵּין יוֹם וּבֵין לָיְלָה.
Thank You for helping us **understand the difference** between day and night, good and otherwise.

3

eev·reem   po·kay·ach   Ah·tuh...   Bo·ruch
בָּרוּךְ אַתָּה... פּוֹקֵחַ עִוְרִים.
Thank You for giving us the **insight** to **see** what is right for us.

4

a·su·reem   ma·teer   Ah·tuh...   Bo·ruch
בָּרוּךְ אַתָּה... מַתִּיר אֲסוּרִים.
Thank You for **enabling us** to do what is right.

5

k'fu·feem   zo·kayf   Ah·tuh...   Bo·ruch
בָּרוּךְ אַתָּה... זוֹקֵף כְּפוּפִים.
Thank You for removing our burdens from us; thank you for allowing us to **stand upright**.

6

a·ru·meem   mal·beesh   Ah·tuh...   Bo·ruch
בָּרוּךְ אַתָּה... מַלְבִּישׁ עֲרֻמִּים.
Thank You for our **clothes** and for the *mitzvos*, the **clothing** of our *neshama*.

7

ko·ach   la·yuh·ayf   ha·no·sayn   Ah·tuh...   Bo·ruch
בָּרוּךְ אַתָּה... הַנּוֹתֵן לַיָּעֵף כֹּחַ.
Thank You for giving us **strength**.

1
Bo·ruch   Ah·tuh...   ro·ka   huh·uh·retz   al   ha·muh·yeem
בָּרוּךְ אַתָּה... רוֹקַע הָאָרֶץ עַל הַמָּיִם.
Thank You for keeping the populated world safe from the **waters** of the oceans.

2
Bo·ruch   Ah·tuh...   ha·may·cheen   meetz·ah·day   guh·vehr
בָּרוּךְ אַתָּה... הַמֵּכִין מִצְעֲדֵי גָבֶר.
Thank you for enabling us to **walk**, and our bodies to work.
Thank You for **guiding** our steps with *hashgacha pratis* so we end up where we need to be.

3
Bo·ruch   Ah·tuh...   sheh·uh·suh   li   kuhl   tzuhr·ki
בָּרוּךְ אַתָּה... שֶׁעָשָׂה לִי כָּל צָרְכִּי.
Thank You for giving me **everything I need**, right down to my shoelaces!

4
Bo·ruch   Ah·tuh...   o·zayr   Yisroel   beeg·vu·ruh
בָּרוּךְ אַתָּה... אוֹזֵר יִשְׂרָאֵל בִּגְבוּרָה.
Thank You for empowering us with the **might** we need in all areas of our life.

5
Bo·ruch   Ah·tuh...   o·tayr   Yisroel   b'seef·uh·ruh
בָּרוּךְ אַתָּה... עוֹטֵר יִשְׂרָאֵל בְּתִפְאָרָה.
Thank You for crowning us with **glory** (including our *kipos*).

6
Bo·ruch   Ah·tuh...   sheh·lo   uh·sa·ni   goy
בָּרוּךְ אַתָּה... שֶׁלֹּא עָשַׂנִי גּוֹי.
Thank You for selecting me as part of **Your chosen nation**, giving me the opportunity to fulfill the *mitzvos*.

7
Bo·ruch   Ah·tuh...   sheh·lo   uh·sa·ni   uh·ved
בָּרוּךְ אַתָּה... שֶׁלֹּא עָשַׂנִי עָבֶד.
Thank You for helping me **free myself** from being a "slave" to my desires and instincts.

8
Bo·ruch   Ah·tuh...   sheh·lo   uh·sa·ni   ee·shuh
בָּרוּךְ אַתָּה... שֶׁלֹּא עָשַׂנִי אִשָּׁה.
Boys: Thank You for giving me the **opportunity** and **responsibility** to fulfill more *mitzvos*.

HAMA'AVIR SHAYNA

Please Hashem, help us overcome
the temptations of the day.

1

Bo·ruch	Ah·tuh	Adonoy	Elohaynu	Meh·lech	huh·o·lum
בָּרוּךְ	אַתָּה	יְיָ,	אֱלֹהֵינוּ,	מֶלֶךְ	הָעוֹלָם,

2

ha·ma·ah·veer	shay·nuh	may·ay·nuy	oos·nu·muh	may·af·ah·poy
הַמַּעֲבִיר	שֵׁנָה	מֵעֵינָי,	וּתְנוּמָה	מֵעַפְעַפָּי.

Thank You for removing sleep from my eyes and slumber from my eyelids,
alerting me to the tricks and dangers of my own *Yetzer Hara*.

3

vi·hee	ruh·tzon	mi·l'fuh·ne·chuh	Adonuy	Elohaynu	vAylohay	a·vo·say·nu
וִיהִי	רָצוֹן	מִלְּפָנֶיךָ,	יְיָ	אֱלֹהֵינוּ	וֵאלֹהֵי	אֲבוֹתֵינוּ,

4

sheh·tar·gi·lay·nu	b'So·ruh·seh·chuh	v'sahd·bee·kay·nu	b'meetz·vo·seh·chuh
שֶׁתַּרְגִּילֵנוּ	בְּתוֹרָתֶךָ,	וְתַדְבִּיקֵנוּ	בְּמִצְוֹתֶיךָ,

5

v'al	t'vi·ay·nu	lo	li·day	chayt
וְאַל	תְּבִיאֵנוּ	לֹא	לִידֵי	חֵטְא,

6

v'lo	li·day	a·vay·ruh	v'uh·vohn
וְלֹא	לִידֵי	עֲבֵירָה	וְעָוֹן,

7

v'lo	li·day	ni·suh·yohn	v'lo	li·day	vi·zuh·yohn
וְלֹא	לִידֵי	נִסָּיוֹן,	וְלֹא	לִידֵי	בִזָּיוֹן,

8

v'al	yeesh·loht	buh·nu	yay·tzer	huh·ruh
וְאַל	יִשְׁלוֹט	בָּנוּ	יֵצֶר	הָרָע,

9

v'har·chi·kay·nu	may·uh·dum	ruh	u·may·chuh·vayr	ruh
וְהַרְחִיקֵנוּ	מֵאָדָם	רָע,	וּמֵחָבֵר	רָע,

וְאַל תְּבִיאֵנוּ... נִסָּיוֹן	יֵצֶר הָרָע
Do not test us	evil inclination

1　וְדַבְּקֵנוּ בְּיֵצֶר טוֹב, וּבְמַעֲשִׂים טוֹבִים,
　　v'da·b'kay·nu　b'yay·tzer　tov　oov·ma·ah·seem　toh·veem

2　וְכוֹף אֶת יִצְרֵנוּ לְהִשְׁתַּעְבֶּד לָךְ,
　　v'chof　es　yeetz·ray·nu　l'heesh·ta·bed　luch

3　וּתְנֵנוּ הַיּוֹם, וּבְכָל יוֹם,
　　oos·nay·nu　ha·yohm　oov·chuhl　yohm

4　לְחֵן, וּלְחֶסֶד, וּלְרַחֲמִים,
　　l'chayn　ool·che·sed　ool·ra·cha·meem

5　בְּעֵינֶיךָ וּבְעֵינֵי כָל רוֹאֵינוּ,
　　b'ay·ne·chuh　oov·ay·nay　chuhl　ro·ay·nu

6　וְתִגְמְלֵנוּ חֲסָדִים טוֹבִים.
　　v'seeg·m'lay·nu　cha·suh·deem　toh·veem

7　בָּרוּךְ אַתָּה יְיָ,
　　Bo·ruch　Ah·tuh　Adonuy

8　הַגּוֹמֵל חֲסָדִים טוֹבִים לְעַמּוֹ יִשְׂרָאֵל.
　　ha·go·mayl　cha·suh·deem　toh·veem　l'a·mo　Yisroel

וּלְרַחֲמִים	וּלְחֶסֶד	לְחֵן	וּבְמַעֲשִׂים טוֹבִים	בְּיֵצֶר טוֹב
mercy	kindness	grace	good deeds	good inclination

YEHI RATZON

Please Hashem, keep me safe,
spiritually and physically.

1
a·vo·sai · vAylohay · Elohai · Adonuy · mi·l'fuh·ne·chuh · ruh·tzon · y'hee
יְהִי רָצוֹן מִלְפָנֶיךָ יְיָ אֱלֹהַי וֵאלֹהֵי אֲבוֹתַי,

2
yohm · oov·chuhl · ha·yohm · sheh·ta·tzi·lay·ni
שֶׁתַּצִילֵנִי הַיוֹם, וּבְכָל יוֹם,

3
puh·neem · u·may·ah·zoos · fuh·neem · may·ah·zay
מֵעַזֵי פָנִים, וּמֵעַזּוּת פָּנִים,

4
ruh · u·mi·shuh·chayn · ruh · u·may·chuh·vayr · ruh · may·uh·dum
מֵאָדָם רָע, וּמֵחָבֵר רָע, וּמִשָׁכֵן רָע,

5
huh·ruh · may·ah·yeen · ruh · u·mi·peh·ga
וּמִפֶּגַע רָע, מֵעַיִן הָרָע,

6
sheh·ker · may·ay·doos · mi·mal·shi·noos · huh·ruh · mi·luh·shohn
מִלָשׁוֹן הָרָע, מִמַּלְשִׁינוּת, מֵעֵדוּת שֶׁקֶר,

7
may·ah·li·luh · ha·b'ri·yohs · mi·seen·ahs
מִשִׂנְאַת הַבְּרִיוֹת, מֵעֲלִילָה,

8
ruh·eem · u·mi·meek·reem · ruh·eem · may·chuh·luh·yeem · m'shu·nuh · mi·mi·suh
מִמִּיתָה מְשֻׁנָה, מֵחֳלָיִם רָעִים, וּמִמִּקְרִים רָעִים,

9
uh·sheh · deen · u·mi·ba·al · kuh·sheh · mi·deen · ha·mahsh·chees · u·mi·suh·tun
וּמִשָׂטָן הַמַּשְׁחִית, מִדִּין קָשֶׁה, וּמִבַּעַל דִין קָשֶׁה,

10
b'rees · ven · sheh·ay·no · u·vayn · b'rees · ven · sheh·hu · bain
בֵּין שֶׁהוּא בֶן בְּרִית, וּבֵין שֶׁאֵינוֹ בֶן בְּרִית,

11
gay·hee·nohm · shel · u·mi·dee·nuh
וּמִדִּינָה שֶׁל גֵּיהִנֹם.

שֶׁתַּצִילֵנִי
save me

מֵאָדָם רָע
from not good people

וּמִפֶּגַע רָע
and not good things

TORAH BLESSINGS

You give us the opportunity and obligation to learn Torah.
Please Hashem, make our Torah study sweet!

1   Bo·ruch   Ah·tuh   Adonuy   Elohaynu   Meh·lech   huh·o·lum
בָּרוּךְ אַתָּה יְיָ, אֱלֹהֵינוּ, מֶלֶךְ הָעוֹלָם,

2   ah·sher   ki·d'shuh·nu   b'meetz·vo·suv   v'tzi·vuh·nu   al   deev·ray   So·ruh
אֲשֶׁר קִדְּשָׁנוּ בְּמִצְוֹתָיו, וְצִוָּנוּ עַל דִּבְרֵי תוֹרָה.

3   v'ha·ah·rev   nuh   Adonuy   Elohaynu
וְהַעֲרֶב נָא יְיָ אֱלֹהֵינוּ,

4   es   deev·ray   So·ruh·s'chuh   b'fee·nu
אֶת דִּבְרֵי תוֹרָתְךָ בְּפִינוּ,

5   oov·fee   chuhl   a·m'chuh   bays   Yisroel
וּבְפִי כָל עַמְּךָ בֵּית יִשְׂרָאֵל,

6   v'neeh·yeh   a·nach·nu   v'tze·eh·tzuh·ay·nu
וְנִהְיֶה אֲנַחְנוּ וְצֶאֱצָאֵינוּ,

7   v'tze·eh·tzuh·ay   chuhl   a·m'chuh   bays   Yisroel
וְצֶאֱצָאֵי כָל עַמְּךָ בֵּית יִשְׂרָאֵל,

8   ku·luh·nu   yo·d'ay   Sh'meh·chuh   v'lo·m'day   So·ruh·s'chuh   leesh·muh
כֻּלָּנוּ יוֹדְעֵי שְׁמֶךָ, וְלוֹמְדֵי תוֹרָתְךָ לִשְׁמָהּ.

9   Bo·ruch   Ah·tuh   Adonuy   ha·m'la·mayd   Torah   l'a·mo   Yisroel
בָּרוּךְ אַתָּה יְיָ, הַמְלַמֵּד תּוֹרָה לְעַמּוֹ יִשְׂרָאֵל.

וְהַעֲרֶב	דִּבְרֵי תוֹרָתְךָ	וְלוֹמְדֵי תוֹרָתְךָ לִשְׁמָהּ
make sweet	the words of Your Torah	learn Torah for its own sake

TORAH BLESSINGS

1. | Bo·ruch | Ah·tuh | Adonuy | Elohaynu | Meh·lech | huh·o·lum |

בָּרוּךְ אַתָּה יְיָ, אֱלֹהֵינוּ, מֶלֶךְ הָעוֹלָם,

2. | ah·sher | buh·char | buh·nu | mi·kuhl | huh·ah·meem | v'nuh·sahn | luh·nu | es | Torah·so |

אֲשֶׁר בָּחַר בָּנוּ מִכָּל הָעַמִּים, וְנָתַן לָנוּ אֶת תּוֹרָתוֹ.

3. | Bo·ruch | Ah·tuh | Adonuy | no·sayn | ha·Torah |

בָּרוּךְ אַתָּה יְיָ, נוֹתֵן הַתּוֹרָה.

After reciting the Torah blessings, we "sample" Torah study,
with selections from the Written and Oral Torah.

BIRKAS KOHANIM: Hashem blesses us, the Jewish People,
and entrusts the Kohanim with the power to bless us.

Verses from the Written Torah

4. | vai·da·bayr | Adonuy | el | Moshe | lay·mor |

וַיְדַבֵּר יְיָ אֶל מֹשֶׁה לֵּאמֹר,

5. | da·bayr | el | A·ha·rohn | v'el | buh·nuv | lay·mor |

דַּבֵּר אֶל אַהֲרֹן, וְאֶל בָּנָיו לֵאמֹר,

6. | ko | s'vuh·ra·chu | es | b'nay | Yisroel | uh·mor | luh·hem |

כֹּה תְבָרְכוּ אֶת בְּנֵי יִשְׂרָאֵל אָמוֹר לָהֶם:

7. | y'vuh·reh·ch'chuh | Adonuy | v'yeesh·m'reh·chuh |

יְבָרֶכְךָ יְיָ וְיִשְׁמְרֶךָ.

8. | yuh·ayr | Adonuy | puh·nuv | ay·le·chuh | vi·chu·ne·kuh |

יָאֵר יְיָ, פָּנָיו אֵלֶיךָ, וִיחֻנֶּךָּ.

9. | yi·suh | Adonuy | puh·nuv | ay·le·chuh | v'yuh·saym | l'chuh | shuh·lom |

יִשָּׂא יְיָ, פָּנָיו אֵלֶיךָ, וְיָשֵׂם לְךָ שָׁלוֹם.

10. | v'suh·mu | es | Sh'mi | al | b'nay | Yisroel | va·A·ni | A·vuh·ra·chaym |

וְשָׂמוּ אֶת שְׁמִי עַל בְּנֵי יִשְׂרָאֵל, וַאֲנִי אֲבָרְכֵם.

שָׁלוֹם	יִשָּׂא	יָאֵר	יְבָרֶכְךָ	מִכָּל הָעַמִּים	בָּחַר בָּנוּ
peace	raise up	shine	He shall bless you	from all nations	He chose us

EILU DEVORIM: Mitzvos that create a perfect and pleasant society.

A *Mishna* from the Oral Torah

1　אֵלּוּ דְבָרִים שֶׁאֵין לָהֶם שִׁעוּר:
　　ay·lu　d'vuh·reem　sheh·ayn　luh·hem　shi·ur

2　הַפֵּאָה, וְהַבִּכּוּרִים, וְהָרְאָיוֹן,
　　ha·pay·uh　v'ha·bee·ku·reem　v'huh·r'uh·yohn

3　וּגְמִילוּת חֲסָדִים, וְתַלְמוּד תּוֹרָה.
　　u·g'mi·loos　cha·suh·deem　v'sal·mood　Torah

From the *Gemara* (Talmud)

4　אֵלּוּ דְבָרִים שֶׁאָדָם אוֹכֵל פֵּרוֹתֵיהֶם בָּעוֹלָם הַזֶּה,
　　ay·lu　d'vuh·reem　sheh·uh·dum　o·chayl　pay·ro·say·hem　buh·o·lum　ha·ze

5　וְהַקֶּרֶן קַיֶּמֶת לְעוֹלָם הַבָּא, וְאֵלּוּ הֵן:
　　v'ha·ke·ren　ka·yeh·mes　luh·o·lum　ha·buh　v'ay·lu　hayn

6　כִּבּוּד אָב וָאֵם, וּגְמִילוּת חֲסָדִים,
　　ki·bood　uv　vuh·aym　u·g'mi·loos　cha·suh·deem

7　וְהַשְׁכָּמַת בֵּית הַמִּדְרָשׁ שַׁחֲרִית וְעַרְבִית,
　　v'hash·kuh·mas　bays　ha·meed·rush　sha·cha·rees　v'ar·vees

שֶׁאֵין לָהֶם שִׁעוּר	וּגְמִילוּת חֲסָדִים	וְתַלְמוּד תּוֹרָה	כְּבּוּד אָב וָאֵם
without limit	acts of kindness	Torah study	honoring parents

ka·luh v'hach·nuh·sas cho·leem u·vee·kur o·r'cheem v'hach·nuh·sas

1 וְהַכְנָסַת אוֹרְחִים, וּבִקּוּר חוֹלִים, וְהַכְנָסַת כַּלָּה,

t'fee·luh v'ee·yun ha·mays v'hal·vuh·yas

2 וְהַלְוָיַת הַמֵּת, וְעִיּוּן תְּפִלָּה,

la·cha·vay·ro uh·dum sheh·bain shuh·lom va·ha·vuh·ahs

3 וַהֲבָאַת שָׁלוֹם שֶׁבֵּין אָדָם לַחֲבֵרוֹ,

l'eesh·toh eesh u·vayn

4 וּבֵין אִישׁ לְאִשְׁתּוֹ,

ku·lum k'ne·ged Torah v'sal·mood

5 וְתַלְמוּד תּוֹרָה כְּנֶגֶד כֻּלָּם.

וַהֲבָאַת שָׁלוֹם	וּבִקּוּר חוֹלִים	וְהַכְנָסַת אוֹרְחִים
bringing peace	visiting the sick	welcoming guests

TZITZIS — Our uniform and reminder for the Mitzvos (for boys).

We stand, hold all our *tzitzis*, recite this *bracha* and then kiss the *tzitzis*.

huh·o·lum Meh·lech Elohaynu Adonuy Ah·tuh Bo·ruch

6 בָּרוּךְ אַתָּה יְיָ, אֱלֹהֵינוּ, מֶלֶךְ הָעוֹלָם,

tzi·tzees meetz·vas al v'tzi·vuh·nu b'meetz·vo·suv ki·d'shuh·nu ah·sher

7 אֲשֶׁר קִדְּשָׁנוּ בְּמִצְוֹתָיו, וְצִוָּנוּ עַל מִצְוַת צִיצִת.

מִצְוַת צִיצִת
the *mitzvah* of *tzitzis*

TALIS BRACHA   Married men (and some boys after Bar Mitzvah) wear a Talis Gadol during morning prayers, surrounding themselves with a Mitzvah.

Here's how to put on the *talis*:

1. While checking to see that all the strings and knots are intact, recite "*Barchi Nafshi:*"

m'ohd guh·dal·tuh Elohai Adonuy Adonuy es naf·shi buh·r'chi

בָּרְכִי **נַפְשִׁי** אֶת יְיָ, יְיָ אֱלֹהַי גָּדַלְתָּ מְאֹד, 1

kai·ri·uh shuh·ma·yeem no·teh ka·sal·muh ohr o·teh luh·vuhsh·tuh v'huh·duhr hod

הוֹד וְהָדָר לָבָשְׁתָּ. עֹטֶה אוֹר כַּשַּׂלְמָה, נוֹטֶה שָׁמַיִם כַּיְרִיעָה. 2

2. Place the *talis* over your head and hold it up over your shoulders and back.
3. Recite this *bracha*:

huh·o·lum Meh·lech Elohaynu Adonuy Ah·tuh Bo·ruch

בָּרוּךְ אַתָּה יְיָ, אֱלֹהֵינוּ, מֶלֶךְ הָעוֹלָם, 3

b'tzi·tzees l'hees·ah·tayf v'tzi·vuh·nu b'meetz·vo·suv ki·d'shuh·nu ah·sher

אֲשֶׁר קִדְּשָׁנוּ בְּמִצְוֹתָיו, וְצִוָּנוּ לְהִתְעַטֵּף בְּצִיצִת. 4

4. Let the *talis* drape over your head and shoulders. Hold both right corners in your right hand and the left corners in your left hand.
Fling the right corners over your left shoulder. Place the left corners over your heart, below your right hand. Recite the following prayer.

yeh·che·suh·yun k'nuh·fe·chuh b'tzayl uh·dum oov·nay Eloheem chas·d'chuh yuh·kuhr ma

מַה **יָּקָר** חַסְדְּךָ אֱלֹהִים, וּבְנֵי אָדָם בְּצֵל כְּנָפֶיךָ יֶחֱסָיוּן. 5

sahsh·kaym a·duh·ne·chuh v'na·chal bay·se·chuh mi·deh·shen yeer·v'yoon

יִרְוְיֻן מִדֶּשֶׁן בֵּיתֶךָ וְנַחַל עֲדָנֶיךָ תַשְׁקֵם. 6

ohr neer·eh b'or'chuh cha·yeem m'kor ee·m'chuh ki

כִּי עִמְּךָ מְקוֹר חַיִּים, בְּאוֹרְךָ נִרְאֶה אוֹר. 7

layv l'yeesh·ray v'tzeed·kuh·s'chuh l'yo·d'eh·chuh chas·d'chuh m'shoch

מְשׁוֹךְ חַסְדְּךָ לְיֹדְעֶיךָ, וְצִדְקָתְךָ לְיִשְׁרֵי לֵב. 8

5. Bring the right sides of the *talis* back over your right shoulder and fling the left sides over your left shoulder. Now (on a weekday) you are ready to put on the *tefilin*!

TEFILIN BRACHOS   Men and boys aged 13 and up wrap Tefilin every weekday, dedicating mind, heart (emotions) and actions to serve Hashem.

1. Position the *tefilin shel yad* (arm *tefilin*) on your left biceps (if you are right-handed) with the *tefilin* box facing your heart.

2. Recite the *bracha*. (Do not speak until the *shel rosh* [head *tefilin*] is in place.)

huh·o·lum   Meh·lech   Elohaynu   Adonuy   Ah·tuh   Bo·ruch

בָּרוּךְ אַתָּה יְיָ, אֱלֹהֵינוּ, מֶלֶךְ הָעוֹלָם,   1

t'fee·leen   l'huh·ni·ach   v'tzi·vuh·nu   b'meetz·vo·suv   ki·d'shuh·nu   ah·sher

אֲשֶׁר קִדְּשָׁנוּ בְּמִצְוֹתָיו, וְצִוָּנוּ לְהָנִיחַ תְּפִלִּין.   2

3. Tighten the knot and wrap the straps;
Fasten the knot to the *tefilin* box by wrapping twice over the knot and *tefilin*, around your biceps, to create a שׁ. Then wrap seven more times on your arm past the elbow, until just before the wrist bone. Wrap the 8th wrap beyond the wrist bone diagonally across and into the palm. Hold the straps in your palm or let them loose while you don the *tefilin shel rosh*.

4. Place the *tefilin shel rosh* (head *tefilin*) on your head like a crown, lining up its front with your hairline, centered above your forehead. Pull the two straps from the back knot over to the front of your body.

5. Wrap the loose end of the *shel yad* strap around your palm once, then three times around your middle finger: once around the base of the finger, once over the middle, and then once more around the base.

6. It is customary to pray *Shacharis* while wrapped in *tefilin*. When that is not an option, be sure to recite the *Shema* (pages 40–41) while wearing the *tefilin*.

If you mistakenly spoke after the first bracha and before the shel rosh was in place, recite this additional bracha while donning the shel rosh:

huh·o·lum   Meh·lech   Elohaynu   Adonuy   Ah·tuh   Bo·ruch

בָּרוּךְ אַתָּה יְיָ, אֱלֹהֵינוּ, מֶלֶךְ הָעוֹלָם,   3

t'fee·leen   meetz·vas   al   v'tzi·vuh·nu   b'meetz·vo·suv   ki·d'shuh·nu   ah·sher

אֲשֶׁר קִדְּשָׁנוּ בְּמִצְוֹתָיו, וְצִוָּנוּ עַל מִצְוַת תְּפִלִּין.   4

HAREINI MEKABEL

I commit to love and treat others as myself.

[20]

1
ha·ray·ni m'ka·bayl uh·lai meetz·vas ah·say
הֲרֵינִי מְקַבֵּל עָלַי מִצְוַת עֲשֵׂה,

2
shel v'uh·hav·tuh l'ray·ah·chuh kuh·mo·chuh
שֶׁל וְאָהַבְתָּ לְרֵעֲךָ כָּמוֹךָ.

וְאָהַבְתָּ	לְרֵעֲךָ	כָּמוֹךָ
love	your fellow	as yourself

MA TOVU

How wonderful that I can pray in a holy place!
Hashem, please accept my prayers.

[21]

3
ma toh·vu o·huh·le·chuh Ya·ah·kov meesh·k'no·seh·chuh Yisroel
מַה טֹּבוּ אֹהָלֶיךָ יַעֲקֹב, מִשְׁכְּנֹתֶיךָ יִשְׂרָאֵל.

4
va·ah·ni b'rov chas·d'chuh uh·vo vay·seh·chuh
וַאֲנִי בְּרֹב חַסְדְּךָ, אָבֹא בֵיתֶךָ,

5
esh·ta·cha·veh el hay·chal kud·sh'chuh b'yeer·uh·seh·chuh
אֶשְׁתַּחֲוֶה אֶל הֵיכַל קָדְשְׁךָ, בְּיִרְאָתֶךָ.

6
va·ah·ni s'fee·luh·si l'chuh Adonuy ais ruh·tzon
וַאֲנִי תְפִלָּתִי לְךָ יְיָ עֵת רָצוֹן,

7
Eloheem b'ruv chas·deh·chuh a·nay·ni beh·eh·mes yeesh·eh·chuh
אֱלֹהִים בְּרָב חַסְדֶּךָ, עֲנֵנִי בֶּאֱמֶת יִשְׁעֶךָ.

טֹבוּ	אֹהָלֶיךָ	תְפִלָּתִי
good	tent	my prayer

ADON OLAM

During prayer, as we mention Hashem's Holy Name,
we focus on Hashem's infinite eternity,
where past, present and future are all one.

1 neev·ruh y'tzoor kuhl b'teh·rem ← muh·lach ah·sher o·lum A·dohn
   אֲדוֹן עוֹלָם, אֲשֶׁר מָלַךְ, בְּטֶרֶם כָּל יְצוּר נִבְרָא,

2 neek·ruh Sh'mo Meh·lech a·zai kol v'chef·tzo na·ah·suh l'ais
   לְעֵת נַעֲשָׂה בְחֶפְצוֹ כֹּל, אֲזַי מֶלֶךְ שְׁמוֹ נִקְרָא.

3 No·ruh yeem·lohch l'va·doh ha·kol keech·los v'a·cha·ray
   וְאַחֲרֵי כִּכְלוֹת הַכֹּל, לְבַדּוֹ יִמְלֹךְ נוֹרָא.

4 b'seef·uh·ruh yeeh·yeh v'Hu ho·veh v'Hu huh·yuh v'Hu
   וְהוּא הָיָה, וְהוּא הֹוֶה, וְהוּא יִהְיֶה בְּתִפְאָרָה.

5 l'hach·bee·ruh Lo l'hahm·sheel shay·ni v'ayn eh·chud v'Hu
   וְהוּא אֶחָד, וְאֵין שֵׁנִי, לְהַמְשִׁיל לוֹ, לְהַחְבִּירָה.

6 v'ha·mees·ruh huh·ohz v'Lo sach·lees b'li ray·shees b'li
   בְּלִי רֵאשִׁית, בְּלִי תַכְלִית, וְלוֹ הָעֹז וְהַמִּשְׂרָה.

7 tzuh·ruh b'ais chev·li v'tzoor go·ah·li v'chai Ay·li v'Hu
   וְהוּא אֵלִי, וְחַי גֹּאֲלִי, וְצוּר חֶבְלִי בְּעֵת צָרָה.

8 ek·ruh b'yohm ko·si m'nuhs li u·muh·nos ni·si v'Hu
   וְהוּא נִסִּי, וּמָנוֹס לִי, מְנָת כּוֹסִי בְּיוֹם אֶקְרָא.

9 v'uh·ee·ruh ee·shan b'ais ru·chi af·keed b'yuh·doh
   בְּיָדוֹ אַפְקִיד רוּחִי, בְּעֵת אִישָׁן וְאָעִירָה.

10 ee·ruh v'lo li Adonuy g'vi·yuh·si ru·chi v'eem
    וְעִם רוּחִי גְוִיָּתִי, יְיָ לִי וְלֹא אִירָא.

וְלֹא אִירָא	ה' לִי	יִהְיֶה	הֹוֶה	הָיָה	אֲדוֹן
I will not fear	Hashem is with me	will be (future)	is (present)	was (past)	Master

> **KORBAN HaTomid**
>
> Our daily prayers correspond to the daily communal Korbanos in the Beis Hamikdash, which brought us close to Hashem. Today, reading the Korbanos is like we are offering them.

1   וַיְדַבֵּר יְיָ אֶל מֹשֶׁה לֵּאמֹר.
vai·da·bayr · Adonuy · el · Moshe · lay·mor

2   צַו אֶת בְּנֵי יִשְׂרָאֵל וְאָמַרְתָּ אֲלֵהֶם,
tzav · es · b'nay · Yisroel · v'uh·mar·tuh · a·lay·hem

3   אֶת קָרְבָּנִי, לַחְמִי לְאִשַּׁי, רֵיחַ נִיחֹחִי,
es · kuhr·buh·ni · lach·mi · l'ee·shai · ray·ach · ni·cho·chi

4   תִּשְׁמְרוּ לְהַקְרִיב לִי בְּמוֹעֲדוֹ.
teesh·m'ru · l'hak·reev · li · b'mo·ah·doh

5   וְאָמַרְתָּ לָהֶם, זֶה הָאִשֶּׁה אֲשֶׁר תַּקְרִיבוּ לַיְיָ,
v'uh·mar·tuh · luh·hem · zeh · huh·ee·sheh · ah·sher · tak·ri·vu · lAdonuy

6   כְּבָשִׂים בְּנֵי שָׁנָה תְמִימִם, שְׁנַיִם לַיוֹם, עוֹלָה תָמִיד.
k'vuh·seem · b'nay · shuh·nuh · s'mi·meem · sh'na·yeem · la·yohm · o·luh · suh·meed

7   אֶת הַכֶּבֶשׂ אֶחָד תַּעֲשֶׂה בַבֹּקֶר,
es · ha·ke·ves · eh·chud · ta·ah·seh · va·bo·kehr

8   וְאֵת הַכֶּבֶשׂ הַשֵּׁנִי תַּעֲשֶׂה בֵּין הָעַרְבָּיִם.
v'ais · ha·ke·ves · ha·shay·ni · ta·ah·seh · bain · huh·ar·buh·yeem

קָרְבָּנִי	עוֹלָה תָמִיד	בַּבֹּקֶר	בֵּין הָעַרְבַּיִם
My *korban* (sacrifice)	a constant offering	in the morning	in the afternoon

1   l'meen·chuh   so·les   huh·ay·fuh   va·ah·si·rees

וַעֲשִׂירִת הָאֵיפָה סֹלֶת לְמִנְחָה,

2   ha·heen   r'vi·ees   kuh·sees   b'sheh·men   b'lu·luh

בְּלוּלָה בְּשֶׁמֶן כָּתִית, רְבִיעַת הַהִין.

3   lAdonuy   ee·sheh   ni·cho·ach   l'ray·ach   si·nai   b'har   huh·ah·su·yuh   tuh·meed   o·las

עֹלַת תָּמִיד, הָעֲשֻׂיָה בְּהַר סִינַי, לְרֵיחַ נִיחֹחַ אִשֶּׁה לַיְיָ.

4   huh·eh·chud   la·ke·ves   ha·heen   r'vi·ees   v'nees·ko

וְנִסְכּוֹ, רְבִיעַת הַהִין לַכֶּבֶשׂ הָאֶחָד,

5   lAdonuy   shay·chuhr   ne·sech   ha·saych   ba·ko·desh

בַּקֹדֶשׁ הַסֵךְ נֶסֶךְ שֵׁכָר לַיְיָ.

6   huh·ar·buh·yeem   bain   ta·ah·seh   ha·shay·ni   ha·ke·ves   v'ais

וְאֵת הַכֶּבֶשׂ הַשֵּׁנִי, תַּעֲשֶׂה בֵּין הָעַרְבָּיִם,

7   lAdonuy   ni·cho·ach   ray·ach   ee·shay   ta·ah·seh   ooch·nees·ko   ha·bo·kehr   k'meen·chas

כְּמִנְחַת הַבֹּקֶר וּכְנִסְכּוֹ תַּעֲשֶׂה, אִשֵּׁה רֵיחַ נִיחֹחַ לַיְיָ.

8   Adonuy   leef·nay   tzuh·fo·nuh   ha·meez·bay·ach   yeh·rech   al   o·so   v'shuh·chaht

וְשָׁחַט אֹתוֹ עַל יֶרֶךְ הַמִּזְבֵּחַ צָפֹנָה לִפְנֵי יְיָ,

9   suh·veev   ha·meez·bay·ach   al   duh·mo   es   ha·ko·ha·neem   A·ha·rohn   b'nay   v'zuh·r'ku

וְזָרְקוּ בְּנֵי אַהֲרֹן הַכֹּהֲנִים אֶת דָּמוֹ עַל הַמִּזְבֵּחַ סָבִיב.

When praying with a *minyan*, mourners recite *Kaddish d'Rabonon* (page 76).

הַמִּזְבֵּחַ	לְרֵיחַ נִיחֹחַ
the Altar	a pleasing fragrance

Praise and thanks which were recited in the
Beis Hamikdosh after offering the daily korbanos.

a·li·lo·suv · vuh·ah·meem · ho·dee·u · veesh·mo · keer·oo · lAdonuy · ho·du

הוֹדוּ לַיָי, קִרְאוּ בִשְׁמוֹ, הוֹדִיעוּ בָעַמִּים עֲלִילוֹתָיו. 1

neef·l'o·suv · b'chuhl · si·chu · lo · za·m'ru · lo · shi·ru

שִׁירוּ לוֹ, זַמְּרוּ לוֹ, שִׂיחוּ בְּכָל נִפְלְאוֹתָיו... 2

tuh·ray·u · al · u·veen·vi·ai · beem·shi·chuy · ti·g'u · al

אַל תִּגְּעוּ בִמְשִׁיחָי, וּבִנְבִיאַי אַל תָּרֵעוּ. 3

PART II. Illustrating our promised future, this was recited in the
Beis Hamikdosh after offering the evening Korbanos.

y'shu·uh·so · yohm · el · mi·yohm · ba·s'ru · huh·uh·retz · kuhl · lAdonuy · shi·ru

שִׁירוּ לַיָי כָּל הָאָרֶץ, בַּשְּׂרוּ מִיּוֹם אֶל יוֹם יְשׁוּעָתוֹ... 4

bees·hee·luh·seh·chuh · l'heesh·ta·bay·ach · kud·sheh·chuh · l'shaym · l'ho·dos

...לְהוֹדוֹת לְשֵׁם קָדְשֶׁךָ, לְהִשְׁתַּבֵּחַ בִּתְהִלָּתֶךָ... 5

PART III. Hashem hears our prayers, even when we do not have the
Beis Hamikdosh and cannot offer Korbanos.

Hu · Kuh·dosh · rahg·luv · la·ha·dom · v'heesh·ta·cha·vu · Elohaynu · Adonuy · ro·m'mu

רוֹמְמוּ יְיָ אֱלֹהֵינוּ, וְהִשְׁתַּחֲווּ לַהֲדֹם רַגְלָיו, קָדוֹשׁ הוּא... 6

uh·vohn · y'cha·payr · Ra·choom · v'Hu

וְהוּא רַחוּם יְכַפֵּר עָוֹן... 7

kuhr·ay·nu · v'yohm · ya·ah·nay·nu · ha·Meh·lech · ho·shi·uh · Adonuy

יְיָ הוֹשִׁיעָה, הַמֶּלֶךְ יַעֲנֵנוּ בְיוֹם קָרְאֵנוּ. 8

רַחוּם	לְהוֹדוֹת	שִׁירוּ לוֹ	הוֹדוּ לַה'
merciful	to thank	sing to Him	praise Hashem

1. meez·mor sheer cha·nu·kas ha·ba·yees l'Duh·veed
מִזְמוֹר שִׁיר חֲנֻכַּת הַבַּיִת לְדָוִד.

2. a·ro·meem·chuh Adonuy ki dee·li·suh·ni v'lo si·mach·tuh o·y'vai li
אֲרוֹמִמְךָ יְיָ כִּי דִלִּיתָנִי, וְלֹא שִׂמַּחְתָּ אֹיְבַי לִי...

3. Adonuy Meh·lech Adonuy muh·luch Adonuy yeem·loch l'o·lum vuh·ed
יְיָ מֶלֶךְ, יְיָ מָלָךְ, יְיָ יִמְלֹךְ לְעוֹלָם וָעֶד.

4. Adonuy Meh·lech Adonuy muh·luch Adonuy yeem·loch l'o·lum vuh·ed
יְיָ מֶלֶךְ, יְיָ מָלָךְ, יְיָ יִמְלֹךְ לְעוֹלָם וָעֶד.

5. v'huh·yuh Adonuy l'Meh·lech al kuhl huh·uh·retz,
וְהָיָה יְיָ לְמֶלֶךְ עַל כָּל הָאָרֶץ,

6. ba·yohm ha·hu yeeh·yeh Adonuy eh·chud oosh·mo eh·chud.
בַּיוֹם הַהוּא יִהְיֶה יְיָ אֶחָד וּשְׁמוֹ אֶחָד.

7. ho·shi·ay·nu Adonuy Elohaynu v'ka·b'tzay·nu meen ha·go·yeem,
הוֹשִׁיעֵנוּ יְיָ אֱלֹהֵינוּ וְקַבְּצֵנוּ מִן הַגּוֹיִם,

8. l'ho·dos l'shaym kud·sheh·chuh l'heesh·ta·bay·ach bees·hee·luh·seh·chuh...
לְהוֹדוֹת לְשֵׁם קָדְשֶׁךָ, לְהִשְׁתַּבֵּחַ בִּתְהִלָּתֶךָ...

9. la·m'na·tzay·ach been·gi·nos meez·mor sheer.
לַמְנַצֵּחַ בִּנְגִינֹת מִזְמוֹר שִׁיר.

10. Eloheem y'chuh·nay·nu vi·vuh·r'chay·nu yuh·ayr puh·nuv ee·tuh·nu se·luh.
אֱלֹהִים יְחָנֵּנוּ וִיבָרְכֵנוּ, יָאֵר פָּנָיו אִתָּנוּ סֶלָה.

11. luh·da·ahs buh·uh·retz dar·ke·chuh b'chuhl go·yeem y'shu·uh·se·chuh...
לָדַעַת בָּאָרֶץ דַּרְכֶּךָ, בְּכָל גּוֹיִם יְשׁוּעָתֶךָ...

ה' יִמְלֹךְ לְעוֹלָם וָעֶד	ה' מָלָךְ	ה' מֶלֶךְ
Hashem will rule forever	Hashem was King	Hashem is King

| BORUCH SHE'OMAR | Blessing and praise to Hashem, Creator and Manager of the world. |

We stand while holding the two front *tzitzis* in our right hand. We kiss them after the *bracha*.
The following two lines are a mystical introduction to fulfilling our mitzvos of the day.

♪ 24

1   לְשֵׁם יִחוּד קוּדְשָׁא בְּרִיךְ הוּא וּשְׁכִינְתֵּהּ,
l'shaym   yi·chood   kood·shuh   b'reech   Hu   u·sh'cheen·tayh

2   לְיַחֲדָא שֵׁם יָ״ה בּו״ה בְּיִחוּדָא שְׁלִים, בְּשֵׁם כָּל יִשְׂרָאֵל.
l'ya·cha·duh   Shaym   yud kay   b'vuv kay   b'yi·chu·duh   sh'leem   b'shaym   kuhl   Yisroel

♪ 25

3   בָּרוּךְ שֶׁאָמַר וְהָיָה הָעוֹלָם, בָּרוּךְ הוּא,
Bo·ruch   sheh·uh·mar   v'huh·yuh   huh·o·lum   Bo·ruch   Hu

4   בָּרוּךְ אוֹמֵר וְעוֹשֶׂה, בָּרוּךְ גּוֹזֵר וּמְקַיֵּם,
Bo·ruch   o·mayr   v'o·seh   Bo·ruch   go·zayr   oom·ka·yaym

5   בָּרוּךְ עֹשֶׂה בְרֵאשִׁית,
Bo·ruch   o·seh   v'ray·shees

6   בָּרוּךְ מְרַחֵם עַל הָאָרֶץ,
Bo·ruch   m'ra·chaym   al   huh·uh·retz

7   בָּרוּךְ מְרַחֵם עַל הַבְּרִיּוֹת,
Bo·ruch   m'ra·chaym   al   ha·b'ri·yos

8   בָּרוּךְ מְשַׁלֵּם שָׂכָר טוֹב לִירֵאָיו,
Bo·ruch   m'sha·laym   suh·chuhr   tov   li·ray·av

9   בָּרוּךְ חַי לָעַד, וְקַיָּם לָנֶצַח,
Bo·ruch   chai   luh·ahd   v'ka·yum   luh·ne·tzach

10   בָּרוּךְ פּוֹדֶה וּמַצִּיל, בָּרוּךְ שְׁמוֹ.
Bo·ruch   po·deh   u·ma·tzeel   Bo·ruch   Sh'mo

אוֹמֵר וְעוֹשֶׂה	גּוֹזֵר וּמְקַיֵּם	מְרַחֵם	שָׂכָר	לָנֶצַח
says and does	decrees and fulfills	has mercy	reward	forever

1   Bo·ruch   Ah·tuh   Adonuy   Elohaynu   Meh·lech   huh·o·lum

בָּרוּךְ אַתָּה יְיָ, אֱלֹהֵינוּ, מֶלֶךְ הָעוֹלָם,

2   huh·Ayl   Uv   huh·Ra·cha·mun   ha·m'hu·lul   b'feh   a·mo

הָאֵל, אָב הָרַחֲמָן, הַמְהֻלָּל בְּפֶה עַמּוֹ.

3   m'shu·buch   oom·fo·uhr   beel·shohn   cha·si·duv   va·ah·vuh·duv

מְשֻׁבָּח וּמְפֹאָר, בִּלְשׁוֹן חֲסִידָיו וַעֲבָדָיו,

4   oov·shi·ray   Duh·veed   av·deh·chuh

וּבְשִׁירֵי דָוִד עַבְדֶּךָ.

5   n'ha·lel·chuh   Adonuy   Elohaynu   beesh·vuh·chos   u·veez·mi·ros

נְהַלֶּלְךָ יְיָ אֱלֹהֵינוּ, בִּשְׁבָחוֹת וּבִזְמִרוֹת,

6   n'ga·del·chuh   oon·sha·bay·cha·chuh   oon·fu·ehr·chuh

נְגַדֶּלְךָ, וּנְשַׁבֵּחֲךָ, וּנְפָאֶרְךָ,

7   v'nam·li·ch'chuh   v'naz·keer   Sheem·chuh   Mal·kay·nu   Elohaynu

וְנַמְלִיכְךָ, וְנַזְכִּיר שִׁמְךָ, מַלְכֵּנוּ, אֱלֹהֵינוּ.

8   yuh·cheed   chay   huh·o·luh·meem   Meh·lech

יָחִיד, חֵי הָעוֹלָמִים מֶלֶךְ,

9   m'shu·buch   oom·fo·uhr   ah·day   ahd   Sh'mo   ha·guh·dol

מְשֻׁבָּח וּמְפֹאָר, עֲדֵי עַד שְׁמוֹ הַגָּדוֹל.

10   Bo·ruch   Ah·tuh   Adonuy   Meh·lech   m'hu·lul   ba·teesh·buh·chos

בָּרוּךְ אַתָּה יְיָ, מֶלֶךְ מְהֻלָּל בַּתִּשְׁבָּחוֹת.

וּבִזְמִרוֹת	בִּשְׁבָחוֹת	נְהַלֶּלְךָ	אָב הָרַחֲמָן
and songs	with praises	we will praise You	Merciful Father

MIZMOR L'SODAH

huh·uh·retz kuhl lAdonuy huh·ri·u l'so·duh meez·mor

מִזְמוֹר לְתוֹדָה, הָרִיעוּ לַייָ כָּל הָאָרֶץ.   1

beer·nuh·nuh l'fuh·nuv bo·u b'seem·chuh Adonuy es eev·du

עִבְדוּ אֶת יְיָ בְּשִׂמְחָה, בֹּאוּ לְפָנָיו בִּרְנָנָה...   2

YEHI CHEVOD

b'ma·ah·suv Adonuy yees·mach l'o·lum Adonuy ch'vod y'hee

יְהִי כְבוֹד יְיָ לְעוֹלָם, יִשְׂמַח יְיָ בְּמַעֲשָׂיו.   3

o·lum v'ahd may·a·tuh m'vo·ruch Adonuy shaym y'hee

יְהִי שֵׁם יְיָ מְבֹרָךְ, מֵעַתָּה וְעַד עוֹלָם...   4

yash·chees v'lo uh·vohn y'cha·payr Ra·choom v'Hu

וְהוּא רַחוּם יְכַפֵּר עָוֹן, וְלֹא יַשְׁחִית,   5

cha·muh·so kuhl yuh·eer v'lo a·po l'huh·sheev v'heer·buh

וְהִרְבָּה לְהָשִׁיב אַפּוֹ, וְלֹא יָעִיר כָּל חֲמָתוֹ.   6

kuhr·ay·nu v'yohm ya·a·nay·nu ha·Meh·lech ho·shi·uh Adonuy

יְיָ הוֹשִׁיעָה, הַמֶּלֶךְ יַעֲנֵנוּ בְיוֹם קָרְאֵנוּ.   7

עִבְדוּ אֶת ה' בְּשִׂמְחָה
serve Hashem with joy

| ASHREI | We praise Hashem's wonders, kindness and mercy, from the Tehilim, the Psalms of King David, in א־ב order. |

1   ahsh·ray   yo·sh'vay   vay·seh·chuh   ohd   y'ha·l'lu·chuh   seh·luh

אַשְׁרֵי יוֹשְׁבֵי בֵיתֶךָ, עוֹד יְהַלְלוּךָ סֶּלָה.

2   ahsh·ray   huh·um   sheh·kuh·chuh   lo   ahsh·ray   huh·um   sheh·Adonuy   Elohuv

אַשְׁרֵי הָעָם שֶׁכָּכָה לּוֹ, אַשְׁרֵי הָעָם שֶׁיְיָ אֱלֹהָיו.

3   t'hee·luh   l'Duh·veed

תְּהִלָּה לְדָוִד,

4   a·ro·meem·chuh   Elohai   ha·Meh·lech   va·ah·vuh·r'chuh   Sheem·chuh   l'o·lum   vuh·ed

אֲרוֹמִמְךָ אֱלֹהַי הַמֶּלֶךְ, וַאֲבָרְכָה שִׁמְךָ לְעוֹלָם וָעֶד.

5   b'chuhl   yohm   a·vuh·r'che·kuh   va·ah·ha·l'luh   Sheem·chuh   l'o·lum   vuh·ed

בְּכָל יוֹם אֲבָרְכֶךָ, וַאֲהַלְלָה שִׁמְךָ לְעוֹלָם וָעֶד.

6   guh·dol   Adonuy   oom·hu·lul   m'ohd   v'leeg·du·luh·so   ayn   chay·kehr

גָּדוֹל יְיָ וּמְהֻלָּל מְאֹד, וְלִגְדֻלָּתוֹ אֵין חֵקֶר.

7   dor   l'dor   y'sha·bach   ma·ah·seh·chuh   oog·vu·ro·seh·chuh   ya·gi·du

דּוֹר לְדוֹר יְשַׁבַּח מַעֲשֶׂיךָ, וּגְבוּרֹתֶיךָ יַגִּידוּ.

8   ha·dar   k'vod   ho·deh·chuh   v'deev·ray   neef·l'o·seh·chuh   uh·si·chuh

הֲדַר כְּבוֹד הוֹדֶךָ, וְדִבְרֵי נִפְלְאֹתֶיךָ אָשִׂיחָה.

נִפְלְאֹתֶיךָ	גָּדוֹל	וַאֲבָרְכָה	אַשְׁרֵי
wonders	great	I will bless	happy

1. veh·eh·zooz no·r'o·seh·chuh yo·may·ru oog·du·luh·s'chuh ah·sa·p'reh·nuh
וֶעֱזוּז נוֹרְאֹתֶיךָ יֹאמֵרוּ, וּגְדֻלָּתְךָ אֲסַפְּרֶנָּה.

2. zeh·cher rav tu·v'chuh ya·bee·u v'tzeed·kuh·s'chuh y'ra·nay·nu
זֵכֶר רַב טוּבְךָ יַבִּיעוּ, וְצִדְקָתְךָ יְרַנֵּנוּ.

3. cha·noon v'ra·choom Adonuy eh·rech a·pa·yeem oog·dul chuh·sed
חַנּוּן וְרַחוּם יְיָ, אֶרֶךְ אַפַּיִם, וּגְדָל חָסֶד.

4. tov Adonuy la·kol v'ra·cha·muv al kuhl ma·ah·suv
טוֹב יְיָ לַכֹּל, וְרַחֲמָיו עַל כָּל מַעֲשָׂיו.

5. yo·du·chuh Adonuy kuhl ma·ah·seh·chuh va·cha·si·deh·chuh y'vuh·r'chu·chuh
יוֹדוּךָ יְיָ כָּל מַעֲשֶׂיךָ, וַחֲסִידֶיךָ יְבָרְכוּכָה.

6. k'vod mal·chu·s'chuh yo·may·ru oog·vu·ruh·s'chuh y'da·bay·ru
כְּבוֹד מַלְכוּתְךָ יֹאמֵרוּ, וּגְבוּרָתְךָ יְדַבֵּרוּ.

7. l'ho·dee·ah leev·nay huh·uh·dum g'vu·ro·suv ooch·vod ha·dar mal·chu·so
לְהוֹדִיעַ לִבְנֵי הָאָדָם גְּבוּרֹתָיו, וּכְבוֹד הֲדַר מַלְכוּתוֹ.

8. mal·chu·s'chuh mal·choos kuhl o·luh·meem u·mem·shal·t'chuh b'chuhl dor vuh·dor
מַלְכוּתְךָ, מַלְכוּת כָּל עֹלָמִים, וּמֶמְשַׁלְתְּךָ בְּכָל דֹּר וָדֹר.

9. so·maych Adonuy l'chuhl ha·no·f'leem v'zo·kayf l'chuhl ha·k'fu·feem
סוֹמֵךְ יְיָ לְכָל הַנֹּפְלִים, וְזוֹקֵף לְכָל הַכְּפוּפִים.

מַלְכוּת	טוֹב	וְרַחוּם
kingdom	Good	Merciful

1. ay·nay chol ay·le·chuh y'sa·bay·ru v'Ah·tuh no·sayn luh·hem es uch·lum b'ee·toh

עֵינֵי כָל אֵלֶיךָ יְשַׂבֵּרוּ, וְאַתָּה נוֹתֵן לָהֶם אֶת אָכְלָם בְּעִתּוֹ.

FOCUS

2. po·say·ach es yuh·deh·chuh u·mas·bee·ah l'chuhl chai ruh·tzon

פּוֹתֵחַ אֶת יָדֶךָ, וּמַשְׂבִּיעַ לְכָל חַי רָצוֹן.

3. tza·deek Adonuy b'chuhl d'ruh·chuv v'chuh·seed b'chuhl ma·ah·suv

צַדִּיק יְיָ בְּכָל דְּרָכָיו, וְחָסִיד בְּכָל מַעֲשָׂיו.

4. kuh·rov Adonuy l'chuhl ko·r'uv l'chol ah·sher yeek·ruh·oo·hu veh·eh·mes

קָרוֹב יְיָ לְכָל קֹרְאָיו, לְכֹל אֲשֶׁר יִקְרָאֻהוּ בֶאֱמֶת.

5. r'tzon y'ray·uv ya·ah·seh v'es shav·uh·sum yeesh·ma v'yo·shi·aym

רְצוֹן יְרֵאָיו יַעֲשֶׂה, וְאֶת שַׁוְעָתָם יִשְׁמַע וְיוֹשִׁיעֵם.

6. sho·mayr Adonuy es kuh·l o·ha·vuv v'ais kuhl huh·r'shuh·eem yash·meed

שׁוֹמֵר יְיָ אֶת כָּל אֹהֲבָיו, וְאֵת כָּל הָרְשָׁעִים יַשְׁמִיד.

7. t'hee·las Adonuy y'da·behr pi

תְּהִלַּת יְיָ יְדַבֶּר פִּי,

8. vi·vuh·raych kuhl buh·suhr shaym kud·sho l'o·lum vuh·ed

וִיבָרֵךְ כָּל בָּשָׂר שֵׁם קָדְשׁוֹ לְעוֹלָם וָעֶד.

9. va·ah·nach·nu n'vuh·raych Yuh may·ah·tuh v'ahd o·lum Ha·l'lu·yuh

וַאֲנַחְנוּ נְבָרֵךְ יָהּ, מֵעַתָּה וְעַד עוֹלָם, הַלְלוּיָהּ.

On weekdays, after the Torah reading, continue with concluding prayers (pages 66-75).

אָכְלָם	פּוֹתֵחַ	וּמַשְׂבִּיעַ	צַדִּיק	קָרוֹב	יִשְׁמַע
food	open	satisfy	righteous	near	He listens

HALELUKAH

1
Ha·l'lu·yuh — ha·l'li — naf·shi — es — Adonuy
הַלְלוּיָהּ, הַלְלִי נַפְשִׁי אֶת יְיָ.

2
a·ha·l'luh — Adonuy — b'cha·yuy — a·za·m'ruh — lAylohai — b'o·dee
אֲהַלְלָה יְיָ בְּחַיָּי, אֲזַמְּרָה לֵאלֹהַי בְּעוֹדִי...

3
Ha·l'lu·yuh — ki — tov — za·m'ruh — Elohaynu
הַלְלוּיָהּ, כִּי טוֹב זַמְּרָה אֱלֹהֵינוּ,

4
ki — nuh·eem — nuh·vuh — s'hee·luh
כִּי נָעִים, נָאוָה תְהִלָּה...

5
Ha·l'lu·yuh — ha·l'lu — es — Adonuy — meen — ha·shuh·ma·yeem
הַלְלוּיָהּ, הַלְלוּ אֶת יְיָ מִן הַשָּׁמַיִם,

6
ha·l'lu·hu — ba·m'ro·meem
הַלְלוּהוּ בַּמְּרוֹמִים...

7
Ha·l'lu·yuh — shi·ru — lAdonuy — sheer — chuh·dush
הַלְלוּיָהּ, שִׁירוּ לַיְיָ שִׁיר חָדָשׁ,

8
t'hee·luh·so — beek·hal — cha·si·deem
תְּהִלָּתוֹ בִּקְהַל חֲסִידִים...

הַלְלוּיָ־הּ	הַלְלִי נַפְשִׁי אֶת ה׳	שִׁירוּ לַה׳ שִׁיר חָדָשׁ
praise Hashem	my soul, praise Hashem	sing to Hashem a new song

| HALELUKAH | Praise Hashem with musical instruments and dance.
(This is also the final chapter of Tehilim.) |

1.

הַלְלוּיָה, הַלְלוּ אֵל בְּקָדְשׁוֹ, הַלְלוּהוּ בִּרְקִיעַ עֻזּוֹ.

Ha·l'lu·yuh   ha·l'lu   Ayl   b'kud·sho   ha·l'lu·hu   beer·ki·ah   u·zo

2.

הַלְלוּהוּ בִּגְבוּרֹתָיו, הַלְלוּהוּ כְּרֹב גֻּדְלוֹ.

ha·l'lu·hu   beeg·vu·ro·suv   ha·l'lu·hu   k'rov   gewd·lo

3.

הַלְלוּהוּ בְּתֵקַע שׁוֹפָר, הַלְלוּהוּ בְּנֵבֶל וְכִנּוֹר.

ha·l'lu·hu   b'say·ka   sho·fuhr   ha·l'lu·hu   b'nay·vel   v'chi·nor

4.

הַלְלוּהוּ בְּתֹף וּמָחוֹל, הַלְלוּהוּ בְּמִנִּים וְעֻגָב.

ha·l'lu·hu   b'sof   u·muh·chol   ha·l'lu·hu   b'mi·neem   v'u·guv

5.

הַלְלוּהוּ בְצִלְצְלֵי שָׁמַע, הַלְלוּהוּ בְּצִלְצְלֵי תְרוּעָה.

ha·l'lu·hu   b'tzeel·tz'lay   shuh·ma   ha·l'lu·hu   b'tzeel·tz'lay   s'ru·uh

6.

כֹּל הַנְּשָׁמָה תְּהַלֵּל יָה, הַלְלוּיָה.

kol   ha·n'shuh·muh   t'ha·layl   Yuh   Ha·l'lu·yuh

7.

כֹּל הַנְּשָׁמָה תְּהַלֵּל יָה, הַלְלוּיָה.

kol   ha·n'shuh·muh   t'ha·layl   Yuh   Ha·l'lu·yuh

| וּמָחוֹל
and dance | בְּתֹף
with drums | הַלְלוּיָ-הּ
praise Hashem |

VAYEVARECH DOVID

1

v'uh·mayn — uh·mayn — l'o·lum — Adonuy — Bo·ruch

בָּרוּךְ יְיָ לְעוֹלָם, אָמֵן וְאָמֵן...

2

ha·kuh·hul — kuhl — l'ay·nay — Adonuy — es — Duh·veed — vai·va·rech

וַיְבָרֶךְ דָּוִד אֶת יְיָ, לְעֵינֵי כָּל הַקָּהָל,

3

Duh·veed — va·yo·mehr

וַיֹּאמֶר דָּוִד:

4

uh·vi·nu — Yisroel — Elohay — Adonuy — Ah·tuh — Bo·ruch

בָּרוּךְ אַתָּה יְיָ, אֱלֹהֵי יִשְׂרָאֵל אָבִינוּ,

5

o·lum — v'ahd — may·o·lum

מֵעוֹלָם וְעַד עוֹלָם...

V'CHAROS

6

eh·retz — es — luh·says — ha·b'rees — ee·mo — v'chuh·ros

וְכָרוֹת עִמּוֹ הַבְּרִית, לָתֵת אֶת אֶרֶץ

7

v'ha·geer·guh·shi — v'hai·vu·si — v'ha·p'ri·zi — huh·eh·mo·ri — ha·chi·ti — ha·k'na·a·ni

הַכְּנַעֲנִי, הַחִתִּי, הָאֱמֹרִי, וְהַפְּרִזִּי, וְהַיְבוּסִי, וְהַגִּרְגָּשִׁי,

8

Uh·tuh — tza·deek — ki — d'vuh·reh·chuh — es — va·tuh·kem — l'zar·o — luh·says

לָתֵת לְזַרְעוֹ, וַתָּקֶם אֶת דְּבָרֶיךָ, כִּי צַדִּיק אָתָּה...

וַתָּקֶם אֶת דְּבָרֶיךָ
You fulfilled Your Words

כִּי צַדִּיק אָתָּה
for You are righteous

VAYOSHA *

1   וַיּוֹשַׁע יְיָ בַּיּוֹם הַהוּא, אֶת יִשְׂרָאֵל מִיַּד מִצְרָיִם,

va·yo·sha   Adonuy   ba·yohm   ha·hu   es   Yisroel   mi·yad   meetz·ruh·yeem

2   וַיַּרְא יִשְׂרָאֵל אֶת מִצְרַיִם, מֵת עַל שְׂפַת הַיָּם.

va·yar   Yisroel   es   meetz·ra·yeem   mays   al   s'fas   ha·yum

3   וַיַּרְא יִשְׂרָאֵל אֶת הַיָּד הַגְּדֹלָה,

va·yar   Yisroel   es   ha·yud   ha·g'doh·luh

4   אֲשֶׁר עָשָׂה יְיָ בְּמִצְרַיִם,

ah·sher   uh·suh   Adonuy   b'meetz·ra·yeem

5   וַיִּירְאוּ הָעָם אֶת יְיָ,

va·yi·r'u   huh·um   es   Adonuy

6   וַיַּאֲמִינוּ בַּיְיָ וּבְמֹשֶׁה עַבְדּוֹ.

va·ya·a·mi·nu   bAdonuy   oov·Moshe   av·doh

AZ YASHIR

6   אָז יָשִׁיר מֹשֶׁה וּבְנֵי יִשְׂרָאֵל אֶת הַשִּׁירָה הַזֹּאת לַיְיָ,

uhz   yuh·sheer   Moshe   oov·nay   Yisroel   es   ha·shi·ruh   ha·zos   lAdonuy

7   וַיֹּאמְרוּ לֵאמֹר: אָשִׁירָה לַיְיָ כִּי גָאֹה גָּאָה,

va·yo·m'ru   lay·mor   uh·shi·ruh   lAdonuy   ki   guh·o   guh·uh

8   סוּס וְרֹכְבוֹ רָמָה בַיָּם.

soos   v'ro·ch'vo   ruh·muh   va·yum

9   עָזִּי וְזִמְרָת יָהּ, וַיְהִי לִי לִישׁוּעָה,

uh·zi   v'zeem·rus   Yuh   vai·hee   li   li·shu·uh

10   זֶה אֵלִי וְאַנְוֵהוּ, אֱלֹהֵי אָבִי וַאֲרֹמְמֶנְהוּ...

zeh   Ayli   v'ahn·vay·Hu   Elohay   uh·vi   va·a·ro·m'men·Hu

---

וַיַּאֲמִינוּ בַּה' וּבְמֹשֶׁה עַבְדּוֹ   זֶה אֵ-לִי וְאַנְוֵהוּ

they believed in Hashem and in Moshe, His servant   this is my G-d and I will glorify Him

This closing bracha of Pesukei d'Zimra includes 15 expressions of praise to Hashem.

On Shabbos:

Mal·kay·nu   luh·ahd   Sheem·chuh   yeesh·ta·bach   oov·chayn

1 יִשְׁתַּבַּח שִׁמְךָ לָעַד מַלְכֵּנוּ,   וּבְכֵן

u·vuh·uh·retz   ba·shuh·ma·yeem   v'ha·kuh·dosh   ha·guh·dol   ha·Meh·lech   huh·Ayl

2 הָאֵל, הַמֶּלֶךְ, הַגָּדוֹל, וְהַקָּדוֹשׁ, בַּשָּׁמַיִם וּבָאָרֶץ.

a·vo·say·nu   vAylohay   Elohaynu   Adonoy   nuh·eh   l'chuh   ki

3 כִּי לְךָ נָאֶה יְיָ אֱלֹהֵינוּ וֵאלֹהֵי אֲבוֹתֵינוּ,

vuh·ed   l'o·lum

4 לְעוֹלָם וָעֶד.

u·mem·shuh·luh   ohz   v'zeem·ruh   ha·layl   oosh·vuh·chuh   sheer

5 שִׁיר וּשְׁבָחָה, הַלֵּל וְזִמְרָה, עֹז וּמֶמְשָׁלָה,

v'seef·eh·res   t'hee·luh   oog·vu·ruh   g'du·luh   ne·tzach

6 נֶצַח, גְּדֻלָּה וּגְבוּרָה, תְּהִלָּה וְתִפְאֶרֶת,

u·mal·choos   k'du·shuh

7 קְדֻשָּׁה וּמַלְכוּת.

וְזִמְרָה	הַלֵּל	וּשְׁבָחָה	שִׁיר	
melody	praise	praise	song	

1   בְּרָכוֹת וְהוֹדָאוֹת, לְשִׁמְךָ הַגָּדוֹל וְהַקָּדוֹשׁ,

b'ruh·chos v'ho·duh·ohs, l'Sheem·chuh ha·guh·dol v'ha·kuh·dosh

2   וּמֵעוֹלָם עַד עוֹלָם אַתָּה אֵל.

u·may·o·lum ahd o·lum Ah·tuh Ayl

3   בָּרוּךְ אַתָּה יְיָ,

Bo·ruch Ah·tuh Adonuy

4   אֵל מֶלֶךְ, גָּדוֹל, וּמְהֻלָּל בַּתִּשְׁבָּחוֹת,

Ayl Meh·lech guh·dol oom·hu·lul ba·teesh·buh·chos

5   אֵל הַהוֹדָאוֹת, אֲדוֹן הַנִּפְלָאוֹת,

Ayl ha·ho·duh·ohs A·dohn ha·neef·luh·ohs

6   בּוֹרֵא כָּל הַנְּשָׁמוֹת, רִבּוֹן כָּל הַמַּעֲשִׂים.

bo·ray kuhl ha·n'shuh·mos, Ree·bohn kuhl ha·ma·ah·seem

7   הַבּוֹחֵר בְּשִׁירֵי זִמְרָה,

ha·bo·chayr b'shi·ray zeem·ruh

8   מֶלֶךְ יָחִיד, חֵי הָעוֹלָמִים.

Meh·lech yuh·cheed, chay huh·o·luh·meem

When praying with a *minyan*, the *Chazzan* recites

Half *Kaddish* (page 76) and *Borchu* (below).

מֶלֶךְ יָחִיד	חֵי הָעוֹלָמִים
the only King	the Life of the worlds

BORCHU The Chazzan invites the congregation to join him in blessing.

We bow along with the *Chazzan* while he says *"Borchu."*

Chazzan:

ha·m'vo·ruch   Adonuy   es   buh·r'chu

בָּרְכוּ אֶת יְיָ הַמְּבֹרָךְ.   1

We bow while saying *"Boruch"* and straighten up for *"A-donai."*

Cong. then *Chazzan:*

vuh·ed   l'o·lum   ha·m'vo·ruch   Adonuy   Bo·ruch

בָּרוּךְ יְיָ הַמְּבֹרָךְ לְעוֹלָם וָעֶד.   2

YOTZER OR First blessing before the Shema:
Hashem creates light and darkness, goodness and otherwise.

huh·o·lum   Meh·lech   Elohaynu   Adonuy   Ah·tuh   Bo·ruch

בָּרוּךְ אַתָּה יְיָ, אֱלֹהֵינוּ, מֶלֶךְ הָעוֹלָם,   3

cho·shech   u·vo·ray   or   yo·tzayr

יוֹצֵר אוֹר, וּבוֹרֵא חֹשֶׁךְ,   4

ha·kol   es   u·vo·ray   shuh·lom   o·seh

עֹשֶׂה שָׁלוֹם, וּבוֹרֵא אֶת הַכֹּל.   5

שָׁלוֹם	חֹשֶׁךְ	אוֹר
peace	darkness	light

BLESSINGS OF SHEMA SAMPLINGS

b'ra·cha·meem   uh·le·huh   v'la·duh·reem   luh·uh·retz   ha·may·eer

הַמֵּאִיר לָאָרֶץ וְלַדָּרִים עָלֶיהָ בְּרַחֲמִים,   1

v'ray·shees   ma·a·say   tuh·meed   yohm   b'chuhl   m'cha·daysh   oov·tu·vo

וּבְטוּבוֹ מְחַדֵּשׁ בְּכָל יוֹם תָּמִיד מַעֲשֵׂה בְרֵאשִׁית...   2

---

k'doh·sheem   bo·ray   v'Go·ah·lay·nu   Mal·kay·nu   Tzu·ray·nu   luh·ne·tzach   tees·buh·raych

תִּתְבָּרֵךְ, לָנֶצַח, צוּרֵנוּ, מַלְכֵּנוּ, וְגֹאֲלֵנוּ, בּוֹרֵא קְדוֹשִׁים...   3

Hu   Kuh·dosh   v'ha·No·ruh   ha·Gi·bor   ha·Guh·dol   ha·Meh·lech   huh·Ayl   Shaym   es

אֶת שֵׁם הָאֵל, הַמֶּלֶךְ הַגָּדוֹל, הַגִּבּוֹר וְהַנּוֹרָא, קָדוֹשׁ הוּא...   4

ANGELS' PRAISE   All kinds of angels sing all kinds of praises.
Here, we chant some of the angels' praises.

Tz'vuh·ohs   Adonuy   Kuh·dosh   Kuh·dosh   Kuh·dosh

קָדוֹשׁ קָדוֹשׁ קָדוֹשׁ, יְיָ צְבָאוֹת,   5

k'vo·doh   huh·uh·retz   chuhl   m'lo

מְלֹא כָל הָאָרֶץ כְּבוֹדוֹ.   6

mi·m'ko·mo   Adonuy   k'vod   Bo·ruch

בָּרוּךְ כְּבוֹד יְיָ מִמְּקוֹמוֹ.   7

הָאָרֶץ	מְלֹא	קָדוֹשׁ
the world	fills	holy

LA·KEIL BORUCH

End of the first blessing before Shema:
Hashem continues to create everything, always.

1   luh-Ayl   Bo·ruch   n'ee·mos   yi·tay·nu   luh·Meh·lech   Ayl   chai   v'ka·yum
לָאֵל בָּרוּךְ נְעִימוֹת יִתֵּנוּ, לַמֶּלֶךְ אֵל חַי וְקַיָּם.

2   z'mi·ros   yo·may·ru   v'seesh·buh·chos   yash·mi·u
זְמִרוֹת יֹאמֵרוּ, וְתִשְׁבָּחוֹת יַשְׁמִיעוּ.

3   ki   Hu   l'va·doh   muh·rohm   v'kuh·dosh
כִּי הוּא לְבַדּוֹ, מָרוֹם וְקָדוֹשׁ,

4   po·ayl   g'vu·ros   o·seh   cha·duh·shos   ba·al   meel·chuh·mos
פּוֹעֵל גְּבוּרוֹת, עוֹשֶׂה חֲדָשׁוֹת, בַּעַל מִלְחָמוֹת,

5   zo·ray·ah   tz'duh·kos   matz·mi·ach   y'shu·ohs   bo·ray   r'fu·ohs
זוֹרֵעַ צְדָקוֹת, מַצְמִיחַ יְשׁוּעוֹת, בּוֹרֵא רְפוּאוֹת,

6   no·ruh   s'hee·los   A·dohn   ha·neef·luh·ohs
נוֹרָא תְהִלּוֹת, אֲדוֹן הַנִּפְלָאוֹת,

7   ha·m'cha·daysh   b'tu·vo   b'chuhl   yohm   tuh·meed   ma·ah·say   v'ray·shees
הַמְחַדֵּשׁ בְּטוּבוֹ, בְּכָל יוֹם תָּמִיד, מַעֲשֵׂה בְרֵאשִׁית.

8   kuh·uh·moor   l'o·say   o·reem   g'doh·leem   ki   l'o·lum   chas·doh
כָּאָמוּר: לְעֹשֵׂה אוֹרִים גְּדוֹלִים, כִּי לְעוֹלָם חַסְדּוֹ.

9   Bo·ruch   Ah·tuh   Adonuy   yo·tzayr   ha·m'o·ros
בָּרוּךְ אַתָּה יְיָ, יוֹצֵר הַמְּאוֹרוֹת.

בּוֹרֵא	אֲדוֹן	הַנִּפְלָאוֹת	הַמְחַדֵּשׁ	תָּמִיד
creates	Master	wonders	renews	continuously

AHAVAS OLAM

Second blessing before Shema:
We prepare to awaken our love for Hashem in Shema
by reminding ourselves that Hashem loves us.

1
Elohaynu Adonuy ah·hav·tuh·nu o·lum a·ha·vas
אַהֲבַת עוֹלָם אֲהַבְתָּנוּ יְיָ אֱלֹהֵינוּ,

2
uh·lay·nu chuh·mal·tuh vi·say·ruh g'doh·luh chem·luh
חֶמְלָה גְדוֹלָה וִיתֵרָה חָמַלְתָּ עָלֵינוּ...

3
ha·m'ra·chaym huh·Ra·cha·mun Uv Uh·vi·nu
אָבִינוּ אָב הָרַחֲמָן, הַמְרַחֵם,

4
bee·nuh b'li·bay·nu v'sayn uh·lay·nu nuh ra·chem
רַחֵם נָא עָלֵינוּ, וְתֵן בְּלִבֵּנוּ בִּינָה,

5
v'la·ah·sos leesh·mor u·l'la·mayd leel·mohd leesh·mo·ah ool·hahs·keel l'huh·veen
לְהָבִין, וּלְהַשְׂכִּיל, לִשְׁמֹעַ, לִלְמֹד, וּלְלַמֵּד, לִשְׁמֹר, וְלַעֲשׂוֹת,

6
b'a·ha·vuh Torah·seh·chuh sal·mood deev·ray kuhl es ool·ka·yaym
וּלְקַיֵּם אֶת כָּל דִּבְרֵי תַלְמוּד תּוֹרָתֶךָ בְּאַהֲבָה.

7
b'meetz·vo·seh·chuh li·bay·nu v'da·bayk b'So·ruh·seh·chuh ay·nay·nu v'huh·ayr
וְהָאֵר עֵינֵינוּ בְּתוֹרָתֶךָ, וְדַבֵּק לִבֵּנוּ בְּמִצְוֹתֶיךָ,

8
Sh'meh·chuh es ool·yeer·uh l'a·ha·vuh l'vuh·vay·nu v'ya·chayd
וְיַחֵד לְבָבֵנוּ לְאַהֲבָה וּלְיִרְאָה אֶת שְׁמֶךָ,

9
vuh·ed l'o·lum ni·kuh·shayl v'lo ni·kuh·laym v'lo nay·vosh v'lo
וְלֹא נֵבוֹשׁ, וְלֹא נִכָּלֵם, וְלֹא נִכָּשֵׁל לְעוֹלָם וָעֶד...

10
We gather the *tzitzis* into our left hand.
huh·uh·retz kahn·fos may·ar·ba l'shuh·lom va·ha·vi·ay·nu
וַהֲבִיאֵנוּ לְשָׁלוֹם מֵאַרְבַּע כַּנְפוֹת הָאָרֶץ...

11
b'a·ha·vuh ha·guh·dol l'Sheem·chuh Mal·kay·nu v'kay·rav·tuh·nu
וְקֵרַבְתָּנוּ מַלְכֵּנוּ לְשִׁמְךָ הַגָּדוֹל בְּאַהֲבָה,

12
Sh'meh·chuh es ool·a·ha·vuh ool·ya·ched·chuh l'chuh l'ho·dos
לְהוֹדוֹת לְךָ וּלְיַחֶדְךָ וּלְאַהֲבָה אֶת שְׁמֶךָ.

13
b'a·ha·vuh Yisroel b'a·mo ha·bo·chayr Adonuy Ah·tuh Bo·ruch
בָּרוּךְ אַתָּה יְיָ, הַבּוֹחֵר בְּעַמּוֹ יִשְׂרָאֵל בְּאַהֲבָה.

| אֲהַבְתָּנוּ | וְדַבֵּק לִבֵּנוּ בְּמִצְוֹתֶיךָ | וְקֵרַבְתָּנוּ | הַבּוֹחֵר בְּעַמּוֹ יִשְׂרָאֵל בְּאַהֲבָה |
| You loved us | Attach our hearts to Your *mitzvos* | bring us close | chooses His nation Israel with love |

SHEMA

We proclaim our loyalty to The One Hashem:
Hear O Israel, Hashem is our G-d, Hashem is One.

The *Shema* is our most important declaration and affirmation of Hashem's unity.

As we say the *Shema* we have in mind that we accept Hashem's Torah and *mitzvos* in our lives, and we are ready to live – and if need be, die – for Hashem.

While holding the *tzitzis* in our left hand, we cover our eyes with our right hand in order to say the *Shema* with total concentration.

Sh'ma   Yisroel

שְׁמַע יִשְׂרָאֵל,   1

Adonuy   Elohaynu

יְיָ אֱלֹהֵינוּ,   2

Adonuy   Eh·chud

יְיָ אֶחָד.   3

Shhh... whisper these words.

Bo·ruch   shaym   k'vod   mal·chu·so   l'o·lum   vuh·ed

בָּרוּךְ שֵׁם כְּבוֹד מַלְכוּתוֹ לְעוֹלָם וָעֶד.   4

| V'AHAVTA | Love Hashem until self-sacrifice, study and teach Torah to our children everywhere, wrap Tefilin and post Mezuzos. |

Pause when you get to a dot (·) to separate between the words.

Elohechuh Adonuy ais v'uh·hav·tuh
1 וְאָהַבְתָּ אֵת יְיָ אֱלֹהֶיךָ,

m'o·deh·chuh oov·chuhl naf·sh'chuh oov·chuhl l'vuh·v'chuh b'chuhl
2 בְּכָל · לְבָבְךָ, וּבְכָל נַפְשְׁךָ, וּבְכָל מְאֹדֶךָ.

huh·ay·leh ha·d'vuh·reem v'huh·yu
3 וְהָיוּ הַדְּבָרִים הָאֵלֶּה,

l'vuh·veh·chuh al ha·yohm m'tza·v'chuh Uh·no·chi ah·sher
4 אֲשֶׁר אָנֹכִי מְצַוְּךָ הַיּוֹם, עַל · לְבָבֶךָ.

bum v'dee·bar·tuh l'vuh·ne·chuh v'shi·nan·tum
5 וְשִׁנַּנְתָּם לְבָנֶיךָ, וְדִבַּרְתָּ בָּם,

oov·ku·meh·chuh oov·shuch·b'chuh va·deh·rech oov·lech·t'chuh b'vay·seh·chuh b'sheev·t'chuh
6 בְּשִׁבְתְּךָ בְּבֵיתֶךָ, וּבְלֶכְתְּךָ בַדֶּרֶךְ, וּבְשָׁכְבְּךָ, וּבְקוּמֶךָ.

ay·ne·chuh bain l'toh·tuh·fos v'huh·yu yuh·deh·chuh al l'ohs ook·shar·tum
7 וּקְשַׁרְתָּם לְאוֹת עַל יָדֶךָ, וְהָיוּ לְטֹטָפֹת בֵּין עֵינֶיךָ.

u·veesh·uh·reh·chuh bay·se·chuh m'zu·zos al ooch·sav·tum
8 וּכְתַבְתָּם · עַל מְזֻזוֹת בֵּיתֶךָ, וּבִשְׁעָרֶיךָ.

| מְאֹדֶךָ | נַפְשְׁךָ | לְבָבְךָ | וְאָהַבְתָּ |
| might/money | soul | heart | love |

| מְזֻזוֹת | לְאוֹת | וּקְשַׁרְתָּם | וּבְקוּמֶךָ | וּבְשָׁכְבְּךָ | בַדֶּרֶךְ | בְּבֵיתֶךָ |
| doorposts | sign | wrap them | wake-up time | bedtime | on the road | in your house |

V'HAYA	Rewards and consequences for keeping the Mitzvos.

1 v'huh·yuh / eem / shuh·mo·ah / teesh·m'u
וְהָיָה, אִם שָׁמֹעַ תִּשְׁמְעוּ,

2 meetz·vo·sai / el / ah·sher / Uh·no·chi / m'tza·veh / es·chem / ha·yohm
אֶל מִצְוֹתַי, אֲשֶׁר אָנֹכִי מְצַוֶּה אֶתְכֶם הַיּוֹם,

3 l'a·ha·vuh / es / Adonuy / Elohaychem
לְאַהֲבָה אֶת יְיָ אֱלֹהֵיכֶם,

4 ool·uv·doh / b'chuhl / l'vav·chem / oov·chuhl / naf·sh'chem
וּלְעָבְדוֹ בְּכָל · לְבַבְכֶם, וּבְכָל נַפְשְׁכֶם.

5 v'nuh·sa·ti / m'tar / ar·tz'chem / b'ee·toh / yo·reh / u·mal·kosh
וְנָתַתִּי מְטַר אַרְצְכֶם בְּעִתּוֹ, יוֹרֶה וּמַלְקוֹשׁ.

6 v'uh·saf·tuh / d'guh·ne·chuh / v'si·ro·sh'chuh / v'yeetz·huh·reh·chuh
וְאָסַפְתָּ דְגָנֶךָ, וְתִירֹשְׁךָ, וְיִצְהָרֶךָ.

7 v'nuh·sa·ti / ay·sev / b'suh·d'chuh / leev·hem·teh·chuh
וְנָתַתִּי עֵשֶׂב בְּשָׂדְךָ, לִבְהֶמְתֶּךָ,

8 v'uh·chal·tuh / v'suh·vuh·tuh
וְאָכַלְתָּ, וְשָׂבָעְתָּ.

וְשָׂבָעְתָּ	וְאָכַלְתָּ	מְטַר	וּלְעָבְדוֹ	שָׁמֹעַ
you will be satisfied	you will eat	rain	to serve Him	listen

1   he·shuh·m'ru   luh·chem   pen   yeef·teh   l'vav·chem

הִשָּׁמְרוּ לָכֶם, פֶּן יִפְתֶּה לְבַבְכֶם,

2   v'sar·tem   va·ah·va·d'tem   Eloheem   a·chay·reem

וְסַרְתֶּם, וַעֲבַדְתֶּם אֱלֹהִים אֲחֵרִים,

3   v'heesh·ta·cha·vi·sem   luh·hem

וְהִשְׁתַּחֲוִיתֶם לָהֶם.

4   v'chuh·ruh   ahf   Adonuy   buh·chem

וְחָרָה, אַף יְיָ בָּכֶם,

5   v'uh·tzar   es   ha·shuh·ma·yeem   v'lo   yeeh·yeh   muh·tuhr

וְעָצַר אֶת הַשָּׁמַיִם, וְלֹא יִהְיֶה מָטָר,

6   v'huh·ah·duh·muh   lo   si·tayn   es   y'vu·luh

וְהָאֲדָמָה לֹא תִתֵּן אֶת יְבוּלָהּ,

7   va·ah·va·d'tem   m'hay·ruh   may·al   huh·uh·retz   ha·toh·vuh

וַאֲבַדְתֶּם מְהֵרָה מֵעַל הָאָרֶץ הַטֹּבָה,

8   ah·sher   Adonuy   no·sayn   luh·chem

אֲשֶׁר יְיָ נֹתֵן לָכֶם.

9   v'sahm·tem   es   d'vuh·rai   ay·leh

וְשַׂמְתֶּם אֶת דְּבָרַי אֵלֶּה,

10   al   l'vav·chem   v'al   naf·sh'chem

עַל לְבַבְכֶם, וְעַל נַפְשְׁכֶם.

הִשָּׁמְרוּ	יִפְתֶּה	וְסַרְתֶּם
beware	be tempted	turn away

1

yed·chem   al   l'ohs   o·sum   ook·shar·tem

וּקְשַׁרְתֶּם · אֹתָם לְאוֹת עַל יֶדְכֶם,

2

ay·nay·chem   bain   l'toh·tuh·fos   v'huh·yu

וְהָיוּ לְטוֹטָפֹת, בֵּין עֵינֵיכֶם.

3

bum   l'da·bayr   b'nay·chem   es   o·sum   v'li·ma·d'tem

וְלִמַּדְתֶּם · אֹתָם אֶת בְּנֵיכֶם לְדַבֵּר בָּם,

4

va·deh·rech   oov·lech·t'chuh   b'vay·seh·chuh   b'sheev·t'chuh

בְּשִׁבְתְּךָ בְּבֵיתֶךָ, וּבְלֶכְתְּךָ בַדֶּרֶךְ,

5

oov·ku·meh·chuh   oov·shuch·b'chuh

וּבְשָׁכְבְּךָ וּבְקוּמֶךָ.

6

u·veesh·uh·reh·chuh   bay·se·chuh   m'zu·zos   al   ooch·sav·tum

וּכְתַבְתָּם · עַל מְזֻזוֹת בֵּיתֶךָ, וּבִשְׁעָרֶיךָ.

7

huh·ah·duh·muh   al   v'nay·chem   vi·may   y'may·chem   yeer·bu   l'ma·ahn

לְמַעַן יִרְבּוּ יְמֵיכֶם, וִימֵי בְנֵיכֶם, עַל הָאֲדָמָה,

8

luh·hem   luh·says   la·ah·vo·say·chem   Adonuy   neesh·ba   ah·sher

אֲשֶׁר נִשְׁבַּע יְיָ לַאֲבֹתֵיכֶם, לָתֵת לָהֶם,

9

huh·uh·retz   al   ha·shuh·ma·yeem   ki·may

כִּימֵי הַשָּׁמַיִם עַל הָאָרֶץ.

וּכְתַבְתָּם	וְלִמַּדְתֶּם	וּקְשַׁרְתֶּם
write	teach	wrap

| VAYOMER | 1) Tzitzis remind us of the Mitzvos and help us stay on the right path. 2) We remember our redemption from Egypt. |

We hold our *tzitzis*, look at them as we begin "*Vayomer*" and kiss them at the words "*tzitzis*" and "*emes*" (during daylight hours).

1   lay·mor   Moshe   el   Adonuy   va·yo·mer
וַיֹּאמֶר יְיָ אֶל מֹשֶׁה לֵּאמֹר:

2   a·lay·hem   v'uh·mar·tuh   Yisroel   b'nay   el   da·bayr
דַּבֵּר אֶל בְּנֵי יִשְׂרָאֵל, וְאָמַרְתָּ אֲלֵהֶם,

3   l'doh·ro·sum   veeg·day·hem   kan·fay   al   tzi·tzees   luh·hem   v'uh·su
וְעָשׂוּ לָהֶם צִיצִת, עַל כַּנְפֵי בִגְדֵיהֶם לְדֹרֹתָם.

4   t'chay·les   p'seel   ha·kuh·nuf   tzi·tzees   al   v'nuh·s'nu
וְנָתְנוּ עַל צִיצִת הַכָּנָף, פְּתִיל תְּכֵלֶת.

5   o·so   oor·ee·sem   l'tzi·tzees   luh·chem   v'huh·yuh
וְהָיָה לָכֶם לְצִיצִת, וּרְאִיתֶם · אֹתוֹ,

6   o·sum   va·ah·si·sem   Adonuy   meetz·vos   kuhl   es   ooz·char·tem
וּזְכַרְתֶּם · אֶת כָּל מִצְוֹת יְיָ, וַעֲשִׂיתֶם · אֹתָם.

7   ay·nay·chem   v'a·cha·ray   l'vav·chem   a·cha·ray   suh·su·ru   v'lo
וְלֹא תָתוּרוּ אַחֲרֵי לְבַבְכֶם, וְאַחֲרֵי עֵינֵיכֶם,

8   a·cha·ray·hem   zo·neem   ah·tem   ah·sher
אֲשֶׁר אַתֶּם זֹנִים אַחֲרֵיהֶם.

וַעֲשִׂיתֶם	מִצְוֹת	וּזְכַרְתֶּם	וּרְאִיתֶם	הַכָּנָף	צִיצִת
and do them	commandments	remember	see	corner	fringes

1　l'ma·ahn　teez·k'ru　va·ah·si·sem　es　kuhl　meetz·vo·suy
לְמַעַן תִּזְכְּרוּ, וַעֲשִׂיתֶם · אֶת כָּל מִצְוֹתָי,

2　veeh·yi·sem　k'doh·sheem　lAylohaychem
וִהְיִיתֶם קְדֹשִׁים לֵאלֹהֵיכֶם.

3　A·ni　Adonuy　Elohaychem
אֲנִי יְיָ אֱלֹהֵיכֶם,

4　ah·sher　ho·tzay·si　es·chem　may·eh·retz　meetz·ra·yeem
אֲשֶׁר הוֹצֵאתִי אֶתְכֶם · מֵאֶרֶץ מִצְרַיִם,

5　leeh·yos　luh·chem　lAyloheem
לִהְיוֹת לָכֶם לֵאלֹהִים.

6　A·ni　Adonuy　Elohaychem
אֲנִי יְיָ אֱלֹהֵיכֶם,

7　A·ni　Adonuy　Elohaychem　e·mes
אֲנִי יְיָ אֱלֹהֵיכֶם, אֱמֶת;

V'YATZIV　Blessing after the Shema: All that we have just proclaimed is true and certain, treasured and dear, forever and ever.

8　v'ya·tzeev　v'nuh·chon　v'ka·yum　v'yuh·shuhr　v'neh·eh·mun　v'uh·hoov　v'chuh·veev
וְיַצִּיב, וְנָכוֹן, וְקַיָּם, וְיָשָׁר, וְנֶאֱמָן, וְאָהוּב וְחָבִיב,

9　v'nech·mud　v'nuh·eem　v'no·ruh　v'ah·deer　oom·su·kun　oom·ku·buhl
וְנֶחְמָד וְנָעִים, וְנוֹרָא וְאַדִּיר, וּמְתֻקָּן, וּמְקֻבָּל,

10　v'tov　v'yuh·feh　ha·duh·vuhr　ha·zeh　uh·lay·nu　l'o·lum　vuh·ed
וְטוֹב וְיָפֶה, הַדָּבָר הַזֶּה עָלֵינוּ לְעוֹלָם וָעֶד...

תִּזְכְּרוּ	מִצְוֹתָי	קְדֹשִׁים	הוֹצֵאתִי אֶתְכֶם	מִצְרַיִם	אֱמֶת
remember	My commandments	holy	I took you out	of Egypt	truth

EZRAS: Hashem always helps us!

luh·hem	u·mo·shi·ah	muh·gayn	may·o·lum	Hu	Ah·tuh	a·vo·say·nu	ez·ras

1 עֶזְרַת אֲבוֹתֵינוּ אַתָּה הוּא מֵעוֹלָם, מָגֵן וּמוֹשִׁיעַ לָהֶם,

vuh·dor	dor	b'chuhl	a·cha·ray·hem	v'leev·nay·hem

2 וְלִבְנֵיהֶם אַחֲרֵיהֶם, בְּכָל דּוֹר וָדוֹר...

MI CHAMOCHA: There is none like Hashem!

Adonuy	buh·ay·leem	chuh·mo·chuh	mi

3 מִי כָמֹכָה בָּאֵלִם, יְיָ,

ba·ko·desh	ne·duhr	kuh·mo·chuh	mi

4 מִי כָּמֹכָה, נֶאְדָּר בַּקֹּדֶשׁ,

feh·leh	o·say	s'hee·los	no·ruh

5 נוֹרָא תְהִלֹּת עֹשֵׂה פֶלֶא.

SHIRA CHADASHA: Thanks to Hashem for our Geula (redemption) from Egypt.

ha·guh·dol	l'Sheem·chuh	g'u·leem	shi·b'chu	cha·duh·shuh	shi·ruh

6 שִׁירָה חֲדָשָׁה שִׁבְּחוּ גְאוּלִים לְשִׁמְךָ הַגָּדוֹל,

v'uh·m'ru	v'heem·li·chu	ho·du	ku·lum	ya·chad	ha·yum	s'fas	al

7 עַל שְׂפַת הַיָּם, יַחַד כֻּלָּם הוֹדוּ, וְהִמְלִיכוּ, וְאָמְרוּ,

vuh·ed	l'o·lum	yeem·loch	Adonuy

8 יְיָ יִמְלֹךְ, לְעוֹלָם וָעֶד.

Yisroel	K'dosh	Sh'mo	Tz'vuh·ohs	Adonuy	go·ah·lay·nu	v'ne·eh·mar

9 וְנֶאֱמַר: גֹּאֲלֵנוּ יְיָ צְבָאוֹת שְׁמוֹ, קְדוֹשׁ יִשְׂרָאֵל.

Yisroel	guh·al	Adonuy	Ah·tuh	Bo·ruch

10 בָּרוּךְ אַתָּה יְיָ, גָּאַל יִשְׂרָאֵל.

גֹּאֲלֵנוּ	שִׁירָה חֲדָשָׁה	עֹשֵׂה פֶלֶא	מִי כָמֹכָה
our Redeemer	a new song	does wonders	who is like You

| SH'MONEH ESREI/AMIDA | The Amida is the main, silent prayer, with 18 (+1) blessings, divided into 3 parts: Praise, Requests & Thanks. |

Our *tefila* is like a ladder, and the *Amida* is at the top.

1. We express our gratitude to Hashem in *Birchos HaShachar*.
2. We awaken our love and fear of Hashem in Psalms of Praise - *Pesukei d'Zimra*.
3. We affirm our faith in Hashem's unity and accept His *mitzvos* in the *Shema*.
4. We are now ready to stand before the King, Hashem, and request all our needs.

These are the *Amida* blessings:

First 3 Brachos: Praise: 1. Fathers   2. Might   3. Holiness

Middle 13 Brachos: Requests:

1. Knowledge
2. Return
3. Forgiveness
4. Redemption
5. Healing
6. Success
7. Ingathering

8. Justice
9. *Heretics
10. Righteous
11. Jerusalem
12. *Moshiach*
13. Acceptance

Final 3 Brachos: Thanks: 1. Service   2. Thanks   3. Peace

We direct our faces towards the site of the *Beis Hamikdosh* in Jerusalem.
(In most of America, we face east.)
We take three steps back, then three steps forward, put our feet together
and stand at attention, like a soldier before a king.
We bend our knees and bow four times during the *Amida*, as noted:
We bend at "*Boruch*", bow at "*Ata*" and straighten up for "*A-donuy*."

AMIDA / SH'MONEH ESREI — The Amida is the main, silent prayer, with 18 (+1) blessings, divided into 3 parts: Praise, Requests & Thanks.

We ask Hashem to help us speak properly to Him in our Amida, with this introduction:

t'hee·luh·seh·chuh · ya·geed · u·fee · teef·tuch · s'fuh·sai · Adonuy

1 אֲדֹנָי שְׂפָתַי תִּפְתָּח, וּפִי יַגִּיד תְּהִלָּתֶךָ.

---

1. אָבוֹת FATHERS: We bless Hashem, our G-d and the G-d of our forefathers, for His help, kindness and protection.

---

a·vo·say·nu · vAylohay · Elohaynu · Adonuy · Ah·tuh · Bo·ruch

2 בָּרוּךְ אַתָּה יְיָ, אֱלֹהֵינוּ, וֵאלֹהֵי אֲבוֹתֵינוּ,

Ya·ah·kov · vAylohay · Yeetz·chuk · Elohay · Av·ruh·hum · Elohay

3 אֱלֹהֵי אַבְרָהָם, אֱלֹהֵי יִצְחָק, וֵאלֹהֵי יַעֲקֹב.

el·yohn · Ayl · v'ha·no·ruh · ha·gi·bor · ha·guh·dol · huh·Ayl

4 הָאֵל הַגָּדוֹל הַגִּבּוֹר וְהַנּוֹרָא, אֵל עֶלְיוֹן,

uh·vos · chas·day · v'zo·chayr · ha·kol · ko·nay · toh·veem · cha·suh·deem · go·mayl

5 גּוֹמֵל חֲסָדִים טוֹבִים, קוֹנֵה הַכֹּל, וְזוֹכֵר חַסְדֵי אָבוֹת,

b'a·ha·vuh · Sh'mo · l'ma·ahn · v'nay·hem · leev·nay · go·ayl · u·may·vi

6 וּמֵבִיא גוֹאֵל לִבְנֵי בְנֵיהֶם, לְמַעַן שְׁמוֹ, בְּאַהֲבָה.

During the Aseres Y'mei Teshuva, we add:

cha·yeem · Eloheem · l'ma·ahn·chuh · ha·cha·yeem · b'say·fer · v'chuhs·vay·nu · ba·cha·yeem · chuh·faytz · Meh·lech · l'cha·yeem · zuch·ray·nu

7 זָכְרֵנוּ לְחַיִּים, מֶלֶךְ חָפֵץ בַּחַיִּים, וְכָתְבֵנוּ בְּסֵפֶר הַחַיִּים, לְמַעַנְךָ אֱלֹהִים חַיִּים.

---

u·muh·gayn · u·mo·shi·ah · o·zayr · Meh·lech

8 מֶלֶךְ, עוֹזֵר וּמוֹשִׁיעַ, וּמָגֵן.

Av·ruh·hum · muh·gayn · Adonuy · Ah·tuh · Bo·ruch

9 בָּרוּךְ אַתָּה יְיָ, מָגֵן אַבְרָהָם.

בְּנֵיהֶם	גּוֹאֵל	אָבוֹת	וְזוֹכֵר	אַתָּה	בָּרוּךְ
children	redeem	fathers	remember	You	Blessed

2. גְּבוּרוֹת MIGHT: The Almighty Hashem supports us, heals us, and restores life to those who passed away (when Moshiach will come).

♪ 40

Ah·tuh	gi·bor	l'o·lum	Adonuy

1 אַתָּה גִּבּוֹר לְעוֹלָם אֲדֹנָי,

m'cha·yeh	may·seem	Ah·tuh	rav	l'ho·shi·ah

2 מְחַיֶּה מֵתִים אַתָּה, רַב לְהוֹשִׁיעַ,

mo·reed	ha·tuhl	*Summer* →	ma·sheev	huh·ru·ach	u·mo·reed	ha·ge·shem

← Winter

3 מוֹרִיד הַטָּל. מַשִּׁיב הָרוּחַ וּמוֹרִיד הַגֶּשֶׁם.

m'chal·kayl	cha·yeem	b'che·sed	m'cha·yeh	may·seem	b'ra·cha·meem	ra·beem

4 מְכַלְכֵּל חַיִּים בְּחֶסֶד, מְחַיֶּה מֵתִים בְּרַחֲמִים רַבִּים,

so·maych	no·f'leem	v'ro·fay	cho·leem	u·ma·teer	a·su·reem

5 סוֹמֵךְ נוֹפְלִים, וְרוֹפֵא חוֹלִים, וּמַתִּיר אֲסוּרִים,

oom·ka·yaym	eh·mu·nuh·so	li·shay·nay	uh·fuhr

6 וּמְקַיֵּם אֱמוּנָתוֹ לִישֵׁנֵי עָפָר.

mi	chuh·mo·chuh	ba·al	g'vu·ros	u·mi	doh·meh	luch

7 מִי כָמוֹךְ בַּעַל גְּבוּרוֹת, וּמִי דּוֹמֶה לָךְ,

Meh·lech	may·mees	oom·cha·yeh	u·matz·mi·ach	y'shu·uh

8 מֶלֶךְ מֵמִית וּמְחַיֶּה, וּמַצְמִיחַ יְשׁוּעָה.

During the *Aseres Y'mei Teshuva*, we add:

mi	chuh·mo·chuh	Uv	huh·Ra·cha·mun	zo·chayr	y'tzu·ruv	l'cha·yeem	b'ra·cha·meem

9 מִי כָמוֹךְ, אַב הָרַחֲמָן, זוֹכֵר יְצוּרָיו לְחַיִּים, בְּרַחֲמִים.

v'neh·eh·mun	Ah·tuh	l'ha·cha·yos	may·seem

10 וְנֶאֱמָן אַתָּה לְהַחֲיוֹת מֵתִים.

Bo·ruch	Ah·tuh	Adonuy	m'cha·yeh	ha·may·seem

11 בָּרוּךְ אַתָּה יְיָ, מְחַיֶּה הַמֵּתִים.

גִּבּוֹר	מְחַיֶּה מֵתִים	מְכַלְכֵּל חַיִּים	וְנֶאֱמָן
mighty	revives the dead	sustains life	trustworthy

3. קְדוּשָׁה HOLINESS: Hashem is Holy, infinitely removed from this world,
yet chooses to connect to us and makes us His holy nation.

Kuh·dosh   v'Sheem·chuh   Kuh·dosh   Ah·tuh

1   אַתָּה קָדוֹשׁ, וְשִׁמְךָ קָדוֹשׁ,

seh·luh   y'ha·l'lu·chuh   yohm   b'chuhl   ook·doh·sheem

2   וּקְדוֹשִׁים בְּכָל יוֹם יְהַלְלוּךָ סֶּלָה.

ha·Kuh·dosh   huh·Ayl   Adonuy   Ah·tuh   Bo·ruch

3   בָּרוּךְ אַתָּה יְיָ, הָאֵל הַקָּדוֹשׁ.

During the *Aseres Y'mei Teshuva*, we replace "huh·Ayl - הָאֵל" with "ha·Meh·lech - הַמֶּלֶךְ."

קָדוֹשׁ
holy

---

4. דַּעַת KNOWLEDGE: Hashem, grant us wisdom, understanding and knowledge.

bee·nuh   le·eh·nosh   oom·la·mayd   da·ahs   l'uh·dum   cho·nayn   Ah·tuh

4   אַתָּה חוֹנֵן לְאָדָם דַּעַת, וּמְלַמֵּד לֶאֱנוֹשׁ בִּינָה.

vuh·duh·ahs   bee·nuh   chuch·muh   may·ee·t'chuh   chuh·nay·nu

5   חָנֵּנוּ מֵאִתְּךָ חָכְמָה, בִּינָה, וָדָעַת.

ha·duh·ahs   cho·nayn   Adonuy   Ah·tuh   Bo·ruch

6   בָּרוּךְ אַתָּה יְיָ, חוֹנֵן הַדָּעַת.

חָכְמָה	בִּינָה	וְדַעַת
wisdom	understanding	knowledge/application

---

5. תְּשׁוּבָה RETURN: Hashem, return us to Your Torah and service.

♫ 43

ha·shi·vay·nu	Uh·vi·nu	l'So·ruh·seh·chuh	
הֲשִׁיבֵנוּ	אָבִינוּ	לְתוֹרָתֶךָ,	1

v'kuh·r'vay·nu	Mal·kay·nu	la·ah·vo·duh·seh·chuh	
וְקָרְבֵנוּ	מַלְכֵּנוּ	לַעֲבוֹדָתֶךָ,	2

v'ha·cha·zi·ray·nu	bees·shu·vuh	sh'lay·muh	l'fuh·ne·chuh	
וְהַחֲזִירֵנוּ	בִּתְשׁוּבָה	שְׁלֵמָה	לְפָנֶיךָ.	3

Bo·ruch	Ah·tuh	Adonuy	huh·ro·tzeh	bees·shu·vuh	
בָּרוּךְ	אַתָּה	יְיָ,	הָרוֹצֶה	בִּתְשׁוּבָה.	4

הֲשִׁיבֵנוּ	לְתוֹרָתֶךָ	בִּתְשׁוּבָה
return us	to Your Torah	return/repentance

---

6. סְלִיחָה FORGIVENESS: Hashem, forgive us for all our wrongdoings.

♫ 44

s'lach	luh·nu	Uh·vi·nu	ki	chuh·tuh·nu	
סְלַח	לָנוּ	אָבִינוּ,	כִּי	חָטָאנוּ,	5

m'chol	luh·nu	Mal·kay·nu	ki	fuh·shuh·nu	
מְחוֹל	לָנוּ	מַלְכֵּנוּ,	כִּי	פָשַׁעְנוּ,	6

ki	Ayl	tov	v'sa·luch	Uh·tuh	
כִּי	אֵל	טוֹב	וְסַלָּח	אָתָּה.	7

Bo·ruch	Ah·tuh	Adonuy	cha·noon	ha·mar·beh	lees·lo·ach	
בָּרוּךְ	אַתָּה	יְיָ,	חַנּוּן	הַמַּרְבֶּה	לִסְלוֹחַ.	8

סְלַח	לָנוּ
forgive us	

7. גְּאוּלָה REDEMPTION: Hashem, see our plight and redeem us from all suffering.

1
    ri·vay·nu   v'ri·vuh   v'un·yay·nu   nuh   r'ay

רְאֵה נָא בְעָנְיֵנוּ, וְרִיבָה רִיבֵנוּ,

2
    Sh'meh·chuh   l'ma·ahn   m'hay·ruh   oog·uh·lay·nu

וּגְאָלֵנוּ מְהֵרָה לְמַעַן שְׁמֶךָ,

3
    Uh·tuh   chuh·zuk   go·ayl   Ayl   ki

כִּי אֵל גּוֹאֵל חָזָק אָתָּה.

4
    Yisroel   go·ayl   Adonuy   Ah·tuh   Bo·ruch

בָּרוּךְ אַתָּה יְיָ, גּוֹאֵל יִשְׂרָאֵל.

וּגְאָלֵנוּ	בְעָנְיֵנוּ	רְאֵה
redeem us	our suffering	see

8. רְפוּאָה HEALING: Hashem, heal all our illnesses.

5
    v'ni·vuh·shay·uh   ho·shi·ay·nu   v'nay·ruh·fay   Adonuy   r'fuh·ay·nu

רְפָאֵנוּ יְיָ וְנֵרָפֵא, הוֹשִׁיעֵנוּ וְנִוָּשֵׁעָה,

6
    Uh·tuh   s'hee·luh·say·nu   ki

כִּי תְהִלָּתֵנוּ אָתָּה.

7
    ma·ko·say·nu   l'chuhl   sh'lay·muh   oor·fu·uh   a·ru·chuh   v'ha·ah·lay

וְהַעֲלֵה אֲרוּכָה וּרְפוּאָה שְׁלֵמָה לְכָל מַכּוֹתֵינוּ,

8
    Uh·tuh   v'Ra·cha·mun   ne·eh·mun   ro·fay   Meh·lech   Ayl   ki

כִּי אֵל מֶלֶךְ רוֹפֵא נֶאֱמָן וְרַחֲמָן אָתָּה.

9
    Yisroel   a·mo   cho·lay   ro·fay   Adonuy   Ah·tuh   Bo·ruch

בָּרוּךְ אַתָּה יְיָ, רוֹפֵא חוֹלֵי עַמּוֹ יִשְׂרָאֵל.

וּרְפוּאָה שְׁלֵמָה	רְפָאֵנוּ
complete healing	heal us

9. בִּרְכַּת הַשָּׁנִים BLESSING FOR THE YEAR: Hashem, bless us
with all our material needs.

1   בָּרֵךְ עָלֵינוּ יְיָ אֱלֹהֵינוּ, אֶת הַשָּׁנָה הַזֹּאת,
   buh·raych uh·lay·nu Adonuy Elohaynu es ha·shuh·nuh ha·zos

2   וְאֵת כָּל מִינֵי תְבוּאָתָהּ לְטוֹבָה,
   v'ais kuhl mi·nay s'vu·uh·suh l'toh·vuh

3   וְתֵן טַל וּמָטָר לִבְרָכָה ← Winter ／ Summer → וְתֵן בְּרָכָה לִבְרָכָה
   v'sayn b'ruh·chuh tal u·muh·tuhr leev·ruh·chuh
   v'sayn b'ruh·chuh

4   עַל פְּנֵי הָאֲדָמָה, וְשַׂבְּעֵנוּ מִטּוּבֶךָ,
   al p'nay huh·ah·duh·muh v'sa·b'ay·nu mi·tu·veh·chuh

5   וּבָרֵךְ שְׁנָתֵנוּ כַּשָּׁנִים הַטּוֹבוֹת לִבְרָכָה,
   u·vuh·raych sh'nuh·say·nu ka·shuh·neem ha·toh·vos leev·ruh·chuh

6   כִּי אֵל טוֹב וּמֵטִיב אַתָּה, וּמְבָרֵךְ הַשָּׁנִים.
   ki Ayl tov u·may·teev Ah·tuh oom·vuh·raych ha·shuh·neem

7   בָּרוּךְ אַתָּה יְיָ, מְבָרֵךְ הַשָּׁנִים.
   Bo·ruch Ah·tuh Adonuy m'vuh·raych ha·shuh·neem

הָאֲדָמָה	וּמָטָר	טַל	בָּרֵךְ
the earth	rain	dew	bless

10. **קִבּוּץ גָּלִיּוֹת** INGATHERING OF THE EXILES: Hashem, blow the blast of freedom, gather our exiles from all over the world, and bring us back to our Holy Land.

l'chay·ru·say·nu guh·dol b'sho·fuhr t'ka
תְּקַע בְּשׁוֹפָר גָּדוֹל לְחֵרוּתֵנוּ, 1

guh·lu·yo·say·nu l'ka·baytz nays v'suh
וְשָׂא נֵס לְקַבֵּץ גָּלִיּוֹתֵינוּ, 2

l'ar·tzay·nu huh·uh·retz kan·fos may·ar·ba ya·chad v'ka·b'tzay·nu
וְקַבְּצֵנוּ יַחַד מֵאַרְבַּע כַּנְפוֹת הָאָרֶץ לְאַרְצֵנוּ. 3

Yisroel a·mo need·chay m'ka·baytz Adonuy Ah·tuh Bo·ruch
בָּרוּךְ אַתָּה יְיָ, מְקַבֵּץ נִדְחֵי עַמּוֹ יִשְׂרָאֵל. 4

לְאַרְצֵנוּ	גָּלִיּוֹתֵינוּ	לְקַבֵּץ	בְּשׁוֹפָר	תְּקַע
to our land	our exiles	gather	horn	blow

11. **מִשְׁפָּט** JUSTICE: Hashem, restore our spiritual leaders and let true justice rule.

k'va·t'chi·luh v'yo·ah·tzay·nu k'vuh·ri·sho·nuh sho·f'tay·nu huh·shi·vuh
הָשִׁיבָה שׁוֹפְטֵינוּ כְּבָרִאשׁוֹנָה, וְיוֹעֲצֵינוּ כְּבַתְּחִלָּה, 5

va·ah·nuh·chuh yuh·gon mi·meh·nu v'huh·sayr
וְהָסֵר מִמֶּנּוּ יָגוֹן וַאֲנָחָה, 6

l'va·d'chuh Adonuy Ah·tuh uh·lay·nu oom·loch
וּמְלוֹךְ עָלֵינוּ אַתָּה יְיָ לְבַדְּךָ, 7

oov·meesh·puht b'tzeh·dek oov·ra·cha·meem b'che·sed
בְּחֶסֶד וּבְרַחֲמִים, בְּצֶדֶק וּבְמִשְׁפָּט. 8

u·meesh·puht tz'duh·kuh o·hayv Meh·lech Adonuy Ah·tuh Bo·ruch
בָּרוּךְ אַתָּה יְיָ, מֶלֶךְ אוֹהֵב צְדָקָה וּמִשְׁפָּט. 9

During the *Aseres Y'mei Teshuva*, we end with: "ha·Meh·lech ha·meesh·puht" — הַמֶּלֶךְ הַמִּשְׁפָּט

שׁוֹפְטֵינוּ	הָשִׁיבָה
our judges	return

12. **מִינִים** HERETICS: Hashem, let there be no hope for the slanderers and heretics, and may all our enemies' plans fail.

seek·vuh   t'hee   al   v'la·mal·shi·neem
1 וְלַמַּלְשִׁינִים אַל תְּהִי תִקְוָה,

yo·vay·du k'reh·ga ha·zay·deem v'chuhl ha·mi·neem v'chuhl
2 וְכָל הַמִּינִים וְכָל הַזֵּדִים, כְּרֶגַע יֹאבֵדוּ,

yi·kuh·ray·su m'hay·ruh a·m'chuh o·y'vay v'chuhl
3 וְכָל אוֹיְבֵי עַמְּךָ מְהֵרָה יִכָּרֵתוּ,

oos·ma·gayr oos·sha·bayr s'a·kayr m'hay·ruh huh·reesh·uh u·mal·choos
4 וּמַלְכוּת הָרִשְׁעָה מְהֵרָה תְעַקֵּר, וּתְשַׁבֵּר, וּתְמַגֵּר,

v'yuh·may·nu beem·hay·ruh v'sach·ni·ah
5 וְתַכְנִיעַ בִּמְהֵרָה בְיָמֵינוּ.

zay·deem u·mach·ni·ah o·y'veem sho·vayr Adonuy Ah·tuh Bo·ruch
6 בָּרוּךְ אַתָּה יְיָ, שֹׁבֵר אֹיְבִים, וּמַכְנִיעַ זֵדִים.

יִכָּרֵתוּ	אוֹיְבֵי עַמְּךָ	יֹאבֵדוּ	וְלַמַּלְשִׁינִים
be cut off	Your nation's enemies	be destroyed	informers

13. צַדִּיקִים RIGHTEOUS: Hashem, show mercy to the righteous, and reward those who trust in You.

♪ 51

	ha·cha·si·deem	v'al	ha·tza·dee·keem	al
1	עַל הַצַּדִּיקִים וְעַל הַחֲסִידִים,			

	Yisroel	bays	a·m'chuh	zeek·nay	v'al
2	וְעַל זִקְנֵי עַמְּךָ בֵּית יִשְׂרָאֵל,				

	so·f'ray·hem	bays	p'lay·tas	v'al
3	וְעַל פְּלֵיטַת בֵּית סוֹפְרֵיהֶם,			

	v'uh·lay·nu	ha·tzeh·dek	gay·ray	v'al
4	וְעַל גֵּרֵי הַצֶּדֶק, וְעָלֵינוּ,			

	Elohaynu	Adonuy	ra·cha·meh·chuh	nuh	yeh·heh·mu
5	יֶהֱמוּ נָא רַחֲמֶיךָ, יְיָ אֱלֹהֵינוּ,				

	beh·eh·mes	b'Sheem·chuh	ha·bo·t'cheem	l'chuhl	tov	suh·chuhr	v'sayn
6	וְתֵן שָׂכָר טוֹב, לְכָל הַבּוֹטְחִים בְּשִׁמְךָ בֶּאֱמֶת,						

	ee·muh·hem	chel·kay·nu	v'seem
7	וְשִׂים חֶלְקֵנוּ עִמָּהֶם,		

	buh·tuch·nu	v'chuh	ki	nay·vosh	lo	ool·o·lum
8	וּלְעוֹלָם לֹא נֵבוֹשׁ, כִּי בְךָ בָּטָחְנוּ.					

	la·tza·dee·keem	u·meev·tuch	meesh·un	Adonuy	Ah·tuh	Bo·ruch
9	בָּרוּךְ אַתָּה יְיָ, מִשְׁעָן וּמִבְטָח לַצַּדִּיקִים.					

הַבּוֹטְחִים	שָׂכָר	רַחֲמֶיךָ	הַחֲסִידִים	הַצַּדִּיקִים
those who trust	reward	Your mercy	pious	righteous

14. יְרוּשָׁלַיִם JERUSALEM: Hashem, return to Jerusalem and rebuild the Beis Hamikdosh.

<!-- track 52 -->

1. וְלִירוּשָׁלַיִם עִירְךָ בְּרַחֲמִים תָּשׁוּב,
v'li·ru·shuh·la·yeem — ee·r'chuh — b'ra·cha·meem — tuh·shoov

2. וְתִשְׁכּוֹן בְּתוֹכָהּ כַּאֲשֶׁר דִּבַּרְתָּ,
v'seesh·kohn — b'so·chuh — ka·ah·sher — dee·bar·tuh

3. וְכִסֵּא דָוִד עַבְדְּךָ מְהֵרָה בְּתוֹכָהּ תָּכִין,
v'chi·say — Duh·veed — av·d'chuh — m'hay·ruh — b'soh·chuh — tuh·cheen

4. וּבְנֵה אוֹתָהּ בְּקָרוֹב בְּיָמֵינוּ בִּנְיַן עוֹלָם.
oov·nay — o·suh — b'kuh·rov — b'yuh·may·nu — been·yahn — o·lum

5. בָּרוּךְ אַתָּה יְיָ, בּוֹנֵה יְרוּשָׁלַיִם.
Bo·ruch — Ah·tuh — Adonuy — bo·nay — Y'ru·shuh·luh·yeem

בּוֹנֵה יְרוּשָׁלַיִם
Builder of Jerusalem

15. מָשִׁיחַ MOSHIACH: Hashem, bring Moshiach because we await him all day!

<!-- track 53 -->

6. אֶת צֶמַח דָּוִד עַבְדְּךָ מְהֵרָה תַצְמִיחַ,
es — tzeh·mach — Duh·veed — av·d'chuh — m'hay·ruh — satz·mi·ach

7. וְקַרְנוֹ תָּרוּם בִּישׁוּעָתֶךָ,
v'kar·no — tuh·room — bee·shu·uh·seh·chuh

8. כִּי לִישׁוּעָתְךָ קִוִּינוּ כָּל הַיּוֹם.
ki — li·shu·uh·s'chuh — ki·vi·nu — kuhl — ha·yohm

9. בָּרוּךְ אַתָּה יְיָ, מַצְמִיחַ קֶרֶן יְשׁוּעָה.
Bo·ruch — Ah·tuh — Adonuy — matz·mi·ach — ke·ren — y'shu·uh

לִישׁוּעָתְךָ קִוִּינוּ
for Your salvation — we hope

16. שׁוֹמֵעַ תְּפִלָּה ACCEPTANCE: Hashem, please listen to and accept all our prayers!

1. שְׁמַע קוֹלֵנוּ יְיָ אֱלֹהֵינוּ, אָב הָרַחֲמָן, רַחֵם עָלֵינוּ,
sh'ma ko·lay·nu Adonuy Elohaynu Uv huh-Ra·cha·mun ra·chaym uh·lay·nu,

2. וְקַבֵּל בְּרַחֲמִים וּבְרָצוֹן אֶת תְּפִלָּתֵנוּ,
v'ka·bayl b'ra·cha·meem oov·ruh·tzon es t'fee·luh·say·nu,

3. כִּי אֵל שׁוֹמֵעַ תְּפִלּוֹת וְתַחֲנוּנִים אָתָּה,
ki Ayl sho·may·ah t'fee·los v'sa·cha·nu·neem Uh·tuh,

4. וּמִלְּפָנֶיךָ, מַלְכֵּנוּ, רֵיקָם אַל תְּשִׁיבֵנוּ.
u·mil'l'fuh·ne·chuh, Mal·kay·nu ray·kum al t'shi·vay·nu.

5. כִּי אַתָּה שׁוֹמֵעַ תְּפִלַּת כָּל פֶּה.
ki Ah·tuh sho·may·ah t'fee·las kuhl peh.

6. בָּרוּךְ אַתָּה יְיָ, שׁוֹמֵעַ תְּפִלָּה.
Bo·ruch Ah·tuh Adonuy, sho·may·ah t'fee·luh.

17. עֲבוֹדָה SERVICE: Hashem, be pleased with our prayers and service.

7. רְצֵה יְיָ אֱלֹהֵינוּ בְּעַמְּךָ יִשְׂרָאֵל, וְלִתְפִלָּתָם שְׁעֵה,
r'tzay Adonuy Elohaynu b'a·m'chuh Yisroel, v'lees·fee·luh·sum sh'ay,

8. וְהָשֵׁב הָעֲבוֹדָה לִדְבִיר בֵּיתֶךָ,
v'huh·shayv huh·ah·vo·duh leed·veer bay·se·chuh,

9. וְאִשֵּׁי יִשְׂרָאֵל וּתְפִלָּתָם בְּאַהֲבָה תְקַבֵּל בְּרָצוֹן,
v'ee·shay Yisroel oos·fee·luh·sum b'a·ha·vuh s'ka·bayl b'ruh·tzon,

10. וּתְהִי לְרָצוֹן תָּמִיד, עֲבוֹדַת יִשְׂרָאֵל עַמֶּךָ.
oos·hee l'ruh·tzon tuh·meed, a·vo·das Yisroel a·meh·chuh.

On Rosh Chodesh and Chol Hamoed, flip to page 83 for Ya'ale V'yavo.

11. וְתֶחֱזֶינָה עֵינֵינוּ בְּשׁוּבְךָ לְצִיּוֹן בְּרַחֲמִים.
v'seh·che·zeh·nuh ay·nay·nu b'shu·v'chuh l'tzi·yohn b'ra·cha·meem.

12. בָּרוּךְ אַתָּה יְיָ, הַמַּחֲזִיר שְׁכִינָתוֹ לְצִיּוֹן.
Bo·ruch Ah·tuh Adonuy, ha·ma·cha·zeer Sh'chi·nuh·so l'tzi·yohn.

שְׁמַע קוֹלֵנוּ	אַתָּה שׁוֹמֵעַ	תְּפִלַּת כָּל פֶּה	וְהָשֵׁב	הָעֲבוֹדָה	שְׁכִינָתוֹ
listen to our voice	You hear	prayers of every mouth	return	service	Hashem's presence

18. הוֹדָאָה GRATITUDE: Hashem, thank You for Your daily
wonders, miracles and mercy.

We bow at "*Modeem*" and
straighten up for "*A-donai*".

1 מוֹדִים אֲנַחְנוּ לָךְ,
luch a·nach·nu mo·deem

2 שָׁאַתָּה הוּא יְיָ אֱלֹהֵינוּ וֵאלֹהֵי אֲבוֹתֵינוּ לְעוֹלָם וָעֶד.
vuh·ed l'o·lum ah·vo·say·nu vAylohay Elohaynu Adonuy Hu shuh·Ah·tuh

3 צוּר חַיֵּינוּ, מָגֵן יִשְׁעֵנוּ, אַתָּה הוּא לְדוֹר וָדוֹר,
vuh·dor l'dor Hu Ah·tuh yeesh·ay·nu muh·gayn cha·yay·nu tzur

4 נוֹדֶה לְּךָ, וּנְסַפֵּר תְּהִלָּתֶךָ,
t'hee·luh·seh·chuh oon·sa·payr l'chuh no·deh

5 עַל חַיֵּינוּ הַמְּסוּרִים בְּיָדֶךָ,
b'yuh·deh·chuh ha·m'su·reem cha·yay·nu al

6 וְעַל נִשְׁמוֹתֵינוּ הַפְּקוּדוֹת לָךְ,
luch ha·p'ku·dos neesh·mo·say·nu v'al

7 וְעַל נִסֶּיךָ שֶׁבְּכָל יוֹם עִמָּנוּ,
ee·muh·nu yohm sheh·b'chuhl ni·seh·chuh v'al

8 וְעַל נִפְלְאוֹתֶיךָ וְטוֹבוֹתֶיךָ שֶׁבְּכָל עֵת,
ais sheh·b'chuhl v'toh·vo·seh·chuh neef·l'o·seh·chuh v'al

9 עֶרֶב, וָבֹקֶר, וְצָהֳרָיִם.
v'tzu·huh·ruh·yeem vuh·vo·kehr eh·rev

10 הַטּוֹב, כִּי לֹא כָלוּ רַחֲמֶיךָ,
ra·cha·meh·chuh chuh·loo lo ki ha·tov

11 הַמְרַחֵם, כִּי לֹא תַמּוּ חֲסָדֶיךָ,
cha·suh·deh·chuh sa·mu lo ki ha·m'ra·chaym

12 כִּי מֵעוֹלָם קִוִּינוּ לָךְ.
luch ki·vi·nu may·o·lum ki

On *Chanuka* and *Purim*, we add "*V'Al Hanisim*" (page 85) here.

רַחֲמֶיךָ	וְצָהֳרָיִם	וָבֹקֶר	עֶרֶב	נִסֶּיךָ	צוּר	מוֹדִים
Your mercy	afternoon	morning	evening	Your miracles	rock/strength	thanks

---

18. הוֹדָאָה GRATITUDE: continued...

♫ 58

1. v'al · ku·lum
וְעַל כֻּלָּם,

2. yees·buh·raych · v'yees·ro·mum · v'yees·na·say · Sheem·chuh · Mal·kay·nu
יִתְבָּרַךְ, וְיִתְרוֹמָם, וְיִתְנַשֵּׂא, שִׁמְךָ מַלְכֵּנוּ,

3. tuh·meed · l'o·lum · vuh·ed
תָּמִיד לְעוֹלָם וָעֶד.

> During the *Aseres Y'mei Teshuva* we add:
>
> ooch·sov · l'cha·yeem · toh·veem · kuhl · b'nay · v'ri·seh·chuh
> וּכְתוֹב לְחַיִּים טוֹבִים, כָּל בְּנֵי בְרִיתֶךָ.

5. v'chuhl · ha·cha·yeem · yo·du·chuh · seh·luh
וְכָל הַחַיִּים יוֹדוּךָ סֶּלָה,

6. vi·hal'lu · Sheem·chuh · ha·guh·dol · l'o·lum · ki · tov
וִיהַלְלוּ שִׁמְךָ הַגָּדוֹל לְעוֹלָם, כִּי טוֹב,

7. huh·Ayl · y'shu·uh·say·nu · v'ez·ruh·say·nu · seh·luh · huh·Ayl · ha·tov
הָאֵל יְשׁוּעָתֵנוּ וְעֶזְרָתֵנוּ סֶּלָה, הָאֵל הַטּוֹב.

8. Bo·ruch · Ah·tuh · Adonuy
בָּרוּךְ אַתָּה יְיָ,

9. ha·tov · Sheem·chuh · ool·chuh · nuh·eh · l'ho·dos
הַטּוֹב שִׁמְךָ, וּלְךָ נָאֶה לְהוֹדוֹת.

וְכָל הַחַיִּים   יוֹדוּךָ סֶּלָה
all living things   thank You forever

> 19. שָׁלוֹם PEACE: Hashem, our Father, grant peace
> and all good blessings to Your children, for we are united.

1. oov·ruh·chuh — toh·vuh — shuh·lom — seem
שִׂים שָׁלוֹם, טוֹבָה, וּבְרָכָה,

2. v'ra·cha·meem — vuh·che·sed — chayn — cha·yeem
חַיִּים, חֵן, וָחֶסֶד, וְרַחֲמִים,

3. a·meh·chuh — Yisroel — kuhl — v'al — uh·lay·nu
עָלֵינוּ, וְעַל כָּל יִשְׂרָאֵל עַמֶּךָ,

4. puh·ne·chuh — b'or — k'eh·chud — ku·luh·nu — Uh·vi·nu — buh·r'chay·nu
בָּרְכֵנוּ אָבִינוּ, כֻּלָּנוּ כְּאֶחָד, בְּאוֹר פָּנֶיךָ.

5. Elohaynu — Adonuy — luh·nu — nuh·sa·tuh — puh·ne·chuh — v'or — ki
כִּי בְאוֹר פָּנֶיךָ, נָתַתָּ לָּנוּ יְיָ אֱלֹהֵינוּ,

6. che·sed — v'a·ha·vas — cha·yeem — toh·ras
תּוֹרַת חַיִּים, וְאַהֲבַת חֶסֶד,

7. v'shuh·lom — v'cha·yeem — v'ra·cha·meem — oov·ruh·chuh — ootz·duh·kuh
וּצְדָקָה, וּבְרָכָה, וְרַחֲמִים, וְחַיִּים, וְשָׁלוֹם,

8. Yisroel — a·m'chuh — es — l'vuh·raych — b'ay·ne·chuh — v'tov
וְטוֹב בְּעֵינֶיךָ לְבָרֵךְ אֶת עַמְּךָ יִשְׂרָאֵל,

9. beesh·lo·meh·chuh — shuh·uh — oov·chuhl — ais — b'chuhl
בְּכָל עֵת, וּבְכָל שָׁעָה, בִּשְׁלוֹמֶךָ.

During the *Aseres Y'mei Teshuva* we add *"Uv'seifer"* (page 64).

10. ba·shuh·lom — Yisroel — a·mo — es — ha·m'vuh·raych — Adonuy — Ah·tuh — Bo·ruch
בָּרוּךְ אַתָּה יְיָ, הַמְבָרֵךְ אֶת עַמּוֹ יִשְׂרָאֵל בַּשָּׁלוֹם.

שָׁלוֹם	בָּרְכֵנוּ	כְּאֶחָד	בְּכָל עֵת
peace	bless us	as one	at all times

END OF AMIDA

1.   v'go·ah·li   tzu·ri   Adonuy   l'fuh·ne·chuh   li·bee   v'heg·yohn   fee   eem·ray   l'ruh·tzon   yeeh·yu
יִהְיוּ לְרָצוֹן אִמְרֵי פִי, וְהֶגְיוֹן לִבִּי לְפָנֶיךָ, יְיָ צוּרִי וְגוֹאֲלִי.

2.   meer·muh   mi·da·bayr   oos·fuh·sai   may·ruh   l'sho·ni   n'tzor   Elohai
אֱלֹהַי, נְצוֹר לְשׁוֹנִי מֵרָע, וּשְׂפָתַי מִדַּבֵּר מִרְמָה,

3.   teeh·yeh   la·kol   ke·uh·fuhr   v'naf·shi   si·dohm   naf·shi   v'leem·ka·l'lai
וְלִמְקַלְלַי נַפְשִׁי תִדּוֹם, וְנַפְשִׁי כֶּעָפָר לַכֹּל תִּהְיֶה,

4.   naf·shi   teer·dohf   oov·meetz·vo·seh·chuh   b'So·ruh·seh·chuh   li·bee   p'sach
פְּתַח לִבִּי בְּתוֹרָתֶךָ, וּבְמִצְוֹתֶיךָ תִּרְדּוֹף נַפְשִׁי.

5.   ruh·uh   uh·lai   ha·cho·sh'veem   v'chuhl
וְכָל הַחוֹשְׁבִים עָלַי רָעָה,

6.   ma·cha·shav·tum   v'kal·kayl   a·tzuh·sum   huh·fayr   m'hay·ruh
מְהֵרָה הָפֵר עֲצָתָם, וְקַלְקֵל מַחֲשַׁבְתָּם.

7.   doh·cheh   Adonuy   u·mal·ach   ru·ach   leef·nay   k'motz   yeeh·yu
יִהְיוּ כְּמֹץ לִפְנֵי רוּחַ, וּמַלְאַךְ יְיָ דֹּחֶה,

8.   va·ah·nay·ni   y'mi·n'chuh   ho·shi·uh   y'dee·deh·chuh   yay·chuh·l'tzun   l'ma·ahn
לְמַעַן יֵחָלְצוּן יְדִידֶיךָ, הוֹשִׁיעָה יְמִינְךָ, וַעֲנֵנִי.

9.   y'mi·ne·chuh   l'ma·ahn   ah·say   Sh'meh·chuh   l'ma·ahn   ah·say
עֲשֵׂה לְמַעַן שְׁמֶךָ, עֲשֵׂה לְמַעַן יְמִינֶךָ,

10.   k'du·shuh·seh·chuh   l'ma·ahn   ah·say   Torah·seh·chuh   l'ma·ahn   ah·say
עֲשֵׂה לְמַעַן תּוֹרָתֶךָ, עֲשֵׂה לְמַעַן קְדֻשָּׁתֶךָ.

11.   v'go·ah·li   tzu·ri   Adonuy   l'fuh·ne·chuh   li·bee   v'heg·yohn   fee   eem·ray   l'ruh·tzon   yeeh·yu
יִהְיוּ לְרָצוֹן אִמְרֵי פִי, וְהֶגְיוֹן לִבִּי לְפָנֶיךָ, יְיָ צוּרִי וְגוֹאֲלִי.

יְהְיוּ לְרָצוֹן אִמְרֵי פִי	נְצוֹר לְשׁוֹנִי מֵרָע	פְּתַח לִבִּי בְּתוֹרָתֶךָ
may my prayers be desired/accepted	stop my mouth from speaking evil	open my heart to Your Torah

---

BRING PEACE	עֹשֶׂה שָׁלוֹם

We take three steps back, then bow to the left while saying עֹשֶׂה הַשָּׁלוֹם בִּמְרוֹמָיו;
then bow forward while saying הוּא; to the right while saying יַעֲשֶׂה שָׁלוֹם עָלֵינוּ,
and forward again while saying וְעַל כָּל יִשְׂרָאֵל וְאִמְרוּ אָמֵן.

During the *Aseres Y'mei Teshuva* we add "ha-הַ."

1   uh·lay·nu   shuh·lom   ya·ah·seh   Hu   beem·ro·muv   ha·shuh·lom   o·seh
עֹשֶׂה הַשָּׁלוֹם בִּמְרוֹמָיו, הוּא יַעֲשֶׂה שָׁלוֹם עָלֵינוּ,

2   uh·mayn   v'eem·ru   Yisroel   kuhl   v'al
וְעַל כָּל יִשְׂרָאֵל, וְאִמְרוּ אָמֵן.

3   a·vo·say·nu   vAylohay   Elohaynu   Adonuy   mi·l'fuh·ne·chuh   ruh·tzon   y'hee
יְהִי רָצוֹן מִלְּפָנֶיךָ, יְיָ אֱלֹהֵינוּ וֵאלֹהֵי אֲבוֹתֵינוּ,

4   v'yuh·may·nu   beem·hay·ruh   ha·meek·dush   bays   sheh·yi·buh·neh
שֶׁיִּבָּנֶה בֵּית הַמִּקְדָּשׁ בִּמְהֵרָה בְיָמֵינוּ,

5   b'So·ruh·seh·chuh   chel·kay·nu   v'sayn
וְתֵן חֶלְקֵנוּ בְּתוֹרָתֶךָ.

This ends the *Amida*.

On *Rosh Chodesh* and some holidays we say *Hallel*.
When with a *minyan*, the *Chazzan* recites Half *Kaddish* and the Torah is read on certain days.

During the *Aseres Y'mei Teshuva* we add this at the end of "*Seem Shalom*."

6   v'ne·chuh·muh   y'shu·uh   toh·vuh   u·far·nuh·suh   v'shuh·lom   b'ruh·chuh   cha·yeem   oov·say·fehr
וּבְסֵפֶר חַיִּים, בְּרָכָה וְשָׁלוֹם, וּפַרְנָסָה טוֹבָה, יְשׁוּעָה וְנֶחָמָה,

7   l'fuh·ne·chuh   v'ni·kuh·sayv   ni·zuh·chayr   toh·vos   oog·zay·ros
וּגְזֵרוֹת טוֹבוֹת, נִזָּכֵר וְנִכָּתֵב לְפָנֶיךָ,

8   ool·shuh·lom   toh·veem   l'cha·yeem   Yisroel   bays   a·m'chuh   v'chuhl   a·nach·nu
אֲנַחְנוּ, וְכָל עַמְּךָ בֵּית יִשְׂרָאֵל, לְחַיִּים טוֹבִים וּלְשָׁלוֹם.

שֶׁיִּבָּנֶה בֵּית הַמִּקְדָּשׁ
the Holy Temple should be rebuilt

Lam'natzeiach

Psalm 20
A powerful prayer to heal the sick.

♫ 63

1 לַמְנַצֵּחַ מִזְמוֹר לְדָוִד.
lam·na·tzay·ach meez·mor l'Duh·veed

2 יַעַנְךָ יְיָ בְּיוֹם צָרָה, יְשַׂגֶּבְךָ שֵׁם אֱלֹהֵי יַעֲקֹב.
ya·ahn·chuh Adonuy b'yohm tzuh·ruh y'sa·gev·chuh shaym Elohay Ya·ah·kov

3 יִשְׁלַח עֶזְרְךָ מִקֹּדֶשׁ, וּמִצִּיּוֹן יִסְעָדֶךָּ.
yeesh·lach ez·r'chuh mi·ko·desh u·mi·tzi·yohn yees·uh·deh·kuh

4 יִזְכֹּר כָּל מִנְחֹתֶיךָ, וְעוֹלָתְךָ יְדַשְּׁנֶה סֶלָה.
yeez·kor kuhl meen·cho·seh·chuh v'o·luh·s'chuh y'da·sh'neh seh·luh

5 יִתֶּן לְךָ כִלְבָבֶךָ, וְכָל עֲצָתְךָ יְמַלֵּא.
yi·ten l'chuh cheel·vuh·veh·chuh v'chuhl a·tzuh·s'chuh y'ma·lay

6 נְרַנְּנָה בִּישׁוּעָתֶךָ, וּבְשֵׁם אֱלֹהֵינוּ נִדְגֹּל,
n'ra·n'nuh bee·shu·uh·seh·chuh oov·shaym Elohaynu need·gol

7 יְמַלֵּא יְיָ כָּל מִשְׁאֲלוֹתֶיךָ.
y'ma·lay Adonuy kuhl meesh·ah·lo·seh·chuh

8 עַתָּה יָדַעְתִּי, כִּי הוֹשִׁיעַ יְיָ מְשִׁיחוֹ,
ah·tuh yuh·da·ti ki ho·shi·ah Adonuy m'shi·cho

9 יַעֲנֵהוּ מִשְּׁמֵי קָדְשׁוֹ, בִּגְבוּרוֹת יֵשַׁע יְמִינוֹ.
ya·ah·nay·hu mi·sh'may kud·sho beeg·vu·ros yay·sha y'mi·no

10 אֵלֶּה בָרֶכֶב, וְאֵלֶּה בַסּוּסִים,
ay·leh vuh·reh·chev v'ay·leh va·su·seem

11 וַאֲנַחְנוּ בְּשֵׁם יְיָ אֱלֹהֵינוּ נַזְכִּיר.
va·ah·nach·nu b'shaym Adonuy Elohaynu naz·keer

12 הֵמָּה כָּרְעוּ וְנָפָלוּ, וַאֲנַחְנוּ קַמְנוּ וַנִּתְעוֹדָד.
hay·muh kuh·r'u v'nuh·fuh·lu va·ah·nach·nu kam·nu va·nees·o·dud

13 יְיָ הוֹשִׁיעָה, הַמֶּלֶךְ יַעֲנֵנוּ בְיוֹם קָרְאֵנוּ.
Adonuy ho·shi·uh ha·Meh·lech ya·ah·nay·nu v'yohm kuhr·ay·nu

יְמַלֵּא ה' כָּל מִשְׁאֲלוֹתֶיךָ   אֵלֶּה בָרֶכֶב וְאֵלֶּה בַסּוּסִים   וַאֲנַחְנוּ בְּשֵׁם ה' אֱ-לֹקֵינוּ
Hashem will fulfill all your requests   they trust in horses and chariots   but we trust in Hashem our G-d

When praying with a *minyan*, the *Chazzan* recites *Kaddish* (page 76).

SHIR SHEL YOM

Song of the Day,
sung by the Levi'im in the Holy Temple.

SUNDAY

♪ 64

1. ha·yohm   yohm   ri·shon   ba·Shabbos
הַיּוֹם, יוֹם רִאשׁוֹן בְּשַׁבָּת,

2. sheh·bo   huh·yu   hal·vi·yeem   o·m'reem   b'vays   ha·meek·dush
שֶׁבּוֹ הָיוּ הַלְוִיִּם אוֹמְרִים בְּבֵית הַמִּקְדָּשׁ:

3. l'Duh·veed   meez·mor   lAdonuy   huh·uh·retz   oom·lo·uh   tay·vayl   v'yo·sh'vay   vuh
לְדָוִד מִזְמוֹר, לַייָ הָאָרֶץ וּמְלוֹאָהּ, תֵּבֵל וְיֹשְׁבֵי בָהּ...

MONDAY

4. ha·yohm   yohm   shay·ni   ba·Shabbos
הַיּוֹם, יוֹם שֵׁנִי בַּשַּׁבָּת,

5. sheh·bo   huh·yu   hal·vi·yeem   o·m'reem   b'vays   ha·meek·dush
שֶׁבּוֹ הָיוּ הַלְוִיִּם אוֹמְרִים בְּבֵית הַמִּקְדָּשׁ:

6. sheer   meez·mor   li·v'nay   Ko·rach
שִׁיר מִזְמוֹר לִבְנֵי קֹרַח.

7. guh·dol   Adonuy   oom·hu·lul   m'ohd   b'eer   Elohaynu   har   kud·sho
גָּדוֹל יְיָ וּמְהֻלָּל מְאֹד, בְּעִיר אֱלֹהֵינוּ הַר קָדְשׁוֹ...

TUESDAY

8. ha·yohm   yohm   sh'li·shi   ba·Shabbos
הַיּוֹם, יוֹם שְׁלִישִׁי בַּשַּׁבָּת,

9. sheh·bo   huh·yu   hal·vi·yeem   o·m'reem   b'vays   ha·meek·dush
שֶׁבּוֹ הָיוּ הַלְוִיִּם אוֹמְרִים בְּבֵית הַמִּקְדָּשׁ:

10. meez·mor   l'Uh·suf   Eloheem   ni·tzuv   ba·ah·das   Ayl   b'ke·rev   Eloheem   yeesh·poht
מִזְמוֹר לְאָסָף, אֱלֹהִים נִצָּב בַּעֲדַת אֵל, בְּקֶרֶב אֱלֹהִים יִשְׁפֹּט...

יוֹם רִאשׁוֹן Sunday	יוֹם שֵׁנִי Monday	יוֹם שְׁלִישִׁי Tuesday

WEDNESDAY

1 ha·yohm yohm r'vi·ee ba·Shabbos
הַיּוֹם, יוֹם רְבִיעִי בַּשַּׁבָּת,

2 sheh·bo huh·yu hal·vi·yeem o·m'reem b'vays ha·meek·dush
שֶׁבּוֹ הָיוּ הַלְוִיִּם אוֹמְרִים בְּבֵית הַמִּקְדָּשׁ:

3 Ayl n'kuh·mos Adonuy Ayl n'kuh·mos ho·fee·uh
אֵל נְקָמוֹת יְיָ, אֵל נְקָמוֹת הוֹפִיעַ...

THURSDAY

4 ha·yohm yohm cha·mi·shi ba·Shabbos
הַיּוֹם, יוֹם חֲמִישִׁי בַּשַּׁבָּת,

5 sheh·bo huh·yu hal·vi·yeem o·m'reem b'vays ha·meek·dush
שֶׁבּוֹ הָיוּ הַלְוִיִּם אוֹמְרִים בְּבֵית הַמִּקְדָּשׁ:

6 lam·na·tzay·ach al ha·gi·tees l'Uh·suf
לַמְנַצֵּחַ עַל הַגִּתִּית לְאָסָף.

7 har·ni·nu lAyloheem u·zay·nu huh·ri·u lAylohay Ya·ah·kov
הַרְנִינוּ לֵאלֹהִים עוּזֵּנוּ, הָרִיעוּ לֵאלֹהֵי יַעֲקֹב...

FRIDAY

8 ha·yohm yohm shi·shi ba·Shabbos
הַיּוֹם, יוֹם שִׁשִּׁי בַּשַּׁבָּת,

9 sheh·bo huh·yu hal·vi·yeem o·m'reem b'vays ha·meek·dush
שֶׁבּוֹ הָיוּ הַלְוִיִּם אוֹמְרִים בְּבֵית הַמִּקְדָּשׁ:

10 Adonuy muh·luch gay·oos luh·vaysh luh·vaysh Adonuy ohz hees·ah·zuhr
יְיָ מָלָךְ גֵּאוּת לָבֵשׁ, לָבֵשׁ יְיָ, עֹז הִתְאַזָּר,

11 ahf ti·kohn tay·vayl bal ti·moht
אַף תִּכּוֹן תֵּבֵל בַּל תִּמּוֹט...

From *Rosh Chodesh Elul* through *Hoshaana Rabba*, we say *"L'Dovid Hashem Ori"* (page 84).

יוֹם רְבִיעִי	יוֹם חֲמִישִׁי	יוֹם שִׁשִּׁי
Wednesday	Thursday	Friday

EIN KELOKEINU

There is none like our G-d!

	kAdonaynu	ayn	kAylohaynu	ayn

1 אֵין כֵּאלֹהֵינוּ, אֵין כַּאדוֹנֵינוּ,

k'Mo·shi·ay·nu	ayn	k'Mal·kay·nu	ayn

2 אֵין כְּמַלְכֵּנוּ, אֵין כְּמוֹשִׁיעֵנוּ.

chAdonaynu	mi	chAylohaynu	mi

3 מִי כֵאלֹהֵינוּ, מִי כַאדוֹנֵינוּ,

ch'Mo·shi·ay·nu	mi	ch'Mal·kay·nu	mi

4 מִי כְמַלְכֵּנוּ, מִי כְמוֹשִׁיעֵנוּ.

lAdonaynu	no·deh	lAylohaynu	no·deh

5 נוֹדֶה לֵאלֹהֵינוּ, נוֹדֶה לַאדוֹנֵינוּ,

l'Mo·shi·ay·nu	no·deh	l'Mal·kay·nu	no·deh

6 נוֹדֶה לְמַלְכֵּנוּ, נוֹדֶה לְמוֹשִׁיעֵנוּ.

Adonaynu	Bo·ruch	Elohaynu	Bo·ruch

7 בָּרוּךְ אֱלֹהֵינוּ, בָּרוּךְ אֲדוֹנֵינוּ,

Mo·shi·ay·nu	Bo·ruch	Mal·kay·nu	Bo·ruch

8 בָּרוּךְ מַלְכֵּנוּ, בָּרוּךְ מוֹשִׁיעֵנוּ.

Adonaynu	Hu	Ah·tuh	Elohaynu	Hu	Ah·tuh

9 אַתָּה הוּא אֱלֹהֵינוּ, אַתָּה הוּא אֲדוֹנֵינוּ,

Mo·shi·ay·nu	Hu	Ah·tuh	Mal·kay·nu	Hu	Ah·tuh

10 אַתָּה הוּא מַלְכֵּנוּ, אַתָּה הוּא מוֹשִׁיעֵנוּ.

כְּמוֹשִׁיעֵנוּ	כְּמַלְכֵּנוּ	כַּאדוֹנֵינוּ	כֵּא-לֹקֵינוּ	אֵין
like our Savior	like our King	like our Master	like our G-d	there is none

tzi·yohn	t'ra·chaym	suh·koom	Ah·tuh	so·shi·ay·nu	Ah·tuh

אַתָּה תוֹשִׁיעֵנוּ, אַתָּה תָקוּם תְּרַחֵם צִיּוֹן, 1

mo·ayd	vuh	ki	l'che·n'nuh	ais	ki

כִּי עֵת לְחֶנְנָהּ, כִּי בָא מוֹעֵד. 2

a·vo·say·nu	vAylohay	Elohaynu	Adonuy	Hu	Ah·tuh

אַתָּה הוּא יְיָ אֱלֹהֵינוּ, וֵאלֹהֵי אֲבוֹתֵינוּ, 3

ha·sa·meem	k'toh·res	es	l'fuh·ne·chuh	a·vo·say·nu	sheh·heek·ti·ru

שֶׁהִקְטִירוּ אֲבוֹתֵינוּ לְפָנֶיךָ, אֶת קְטֹרֶת הַסַּמִּים. 4

v'ha·l'vo·nuh	ha·chel·b'nuh	v'ha·tzi·po·ren	ha·tzuh·ri	ha·k'toh·res	pi·toom

פִּטּוּם הַקְּטֹרֶת: הַצֳּרִי, וְהַצִּפֹּרֶן, הַחֶלְבְּנָה, וְהַלְּבוֹנָה... 5

ki·nuh·mon	ki·lu·fuh	ha·kohsht	v'char·kom	shi·bo·les nayrd	ook·tzi·uh	mor

מוֹר, וּקְצִיעָה, שִׁבֹּלֶת נֵרְדְּ, וְכַרְכֹּם... הַקֹּשְׁטְ... קִלּוּפָה... קִנָּמוֹן... 6

קְטֹרֶת	מוֹעֵד
incense	appointed time/holiday

LEMA'AN ACHAI   A blessing of peace and strength.

buch	shuh·lom	nuh	a·da·b'ruh	v'ray·uy	a·chai	l'ma·ahn

לְמַעַן אַחַי וְרֵעָי, אֲדַבְּרָה נָּא שָׁלוֹם בָּךְ. 7

luch	tov	a·vak·shuh	Elohaynu	Adonuy	bays	l'ma·ahn

לְמַעַן בֵּית יְיָ אֱלֹהֵינוּ, אֲבַקְשָׁה טוֹב לָךְ. 8

yi·tayn	l'a·mo	ohz	Adonuy

יְיָ עֹז לְעַמּוֹ יִתֵּן, 9

va·shuh·lom	a·mo	es	y'vuh·raych	Adonuy

יְיָ יְבָרֵךְ אֶת עַמּוֹ בַשָּׁלוֹם. 10

When praying with a *minyan*, mourners recite *Kaddish d'Rabonon* (page 76).

עֹז	שָׁלוֹם	וְרֵעָי	אַחַי
strength	peace	my friends	my brothers

| ALEINU | We proclaim Hashem as the Creator and praise Him, thankful that He chose us to be His special people. |

♪ 66

1 uh·lay·nu l'sha·bay·ach la·Adon ha·kol
עָלֵינוּ לְשַׁבֵּחַ לַאֲדוֹן הַכֹּל,

2 luh·says g'du·luh l'yo·tzayr b'ray·shees
לָתֵת גְּדֻלָּה לְיוֹצֵר בְּרֵאשִׁית,

3 sheh·lo uh·suh·nu k'go·yay huh·ah·ruh·tzos
שֶׁלֹּא עָשָׂנוּ כְּגוֹיֵי הָאֲרָצוֹת,

4 v'lo suh·muh·nu k'meesh·p'chos huh·ah·duh·muh
וְלֹא שָׂמָנוּ כְּמִשְׁפְּחוֹת הָאֲדָמָה.

5 sheh·lo sum chel·kay·nu kuh·hem
שֶׁלֹּא שָׂם חֶלְקֵנוּ כָּהֶם,

6 v'go·ruh·lay·nu k'chuhl ha·mo·num
וְגוֹרָלֵנוּ כְּכָל הֲמוֹנָם.

7 sheh·haym meesh·ta·cha·veem l'heh·vel v'luh·reek
שֶׁהֵם מִשְׁתַּחֲוִים לְהֶבֶל וָלָרִיק.

8 va·ah·nach·nu ko·r'eem u·meesh·ta·cha·veem u·mo·deem
וַאֲנַחְנוּ כּוֹרְעִים, וּמִשְׁתַּחֲוִים, וּמוֹדִים:

9 leef·nay Meh·lech Mal·chay ha·m'luh·cheem ha·Kuh·dosh Bo·ruch Hu
לִפְנֵי מֶלֶךְ מַלְכֵי הַמְּלָכִים, הַקָּדוֹשׁ בָּרוּךְ הוּא.

| עָלֵינוּ לְשַׁבֵּחַ | וּמִשְׁתַּחֲוִים | וּמוֹדִים | מֶלֶךְ מַלְכֵי הַמְּלָכִים | הַקָּדוֹשׁ בָּרוּךְ הוּא |
| we must praise | we bow | we thank | the King of kings | the Holy One, Blessed be He |

1   שֶׁהוּא נוֹטֶה שָׁמַיִם, וְיוֹסֵד אָרֶץ,
    sheh·hu   no·teh   shuh·ma·yeem   v'yo·sayd   uh·retz

2   וּמוֹשַׁב יְקָרוֹ בַּשָּׁמַיִם מִמַּעַל,
    u·mo·shav   y'kuh·ro   ba·shuh·ma·yeem   mi·ma·al

3   וּשְׁכִינַת עֻזוֹ בְּגָבְהֵי מְרוֹמִים,
    oosh·chi·nas   u·zo   b'guh·v'hay   m'ro·meem

4   הוּא אֱלֹהֵינוּ, אֵין עוֹד.
    Hu   Elohaynu   ayn   ohd

5   אֱמֶת מַלְכֵּנוּ, אֶפֶס זוּלָתוֹ.
    e·mes   Mal·kay·nu   eh·fes   zu·luh·so

6   כַּכָּתוּב בְּתוֹרָתוֹ:
    ka·kuh·soov   b'So·ruh·so

7   וְיָדַעְתָּ הַיּוֹם, וַהֲשֵׁבֹתָ אֶל לְבָבֶךָ,
    v'yuh·da·tuh   ha·yohm   va·ha·shay·vo·suh   el   l'vuh·veh·chuh

8   כִּי יְיָ הוּא הָאֱלֹהִים,
    ki   Adonuy   Hu   huh·Eloheem

9   בַּשָּׁמַיִם מִמַּעַל, וְעַל הָאָרֶץ מִתָּחַת,
    ba·shuh·ma·yeem   mi·ma·al   v'al   huh·uh·retz   mi·tuh·chas

10   אֵין עוֹד.
    ayn   ohd

אֱמֶת מַלְכֵּנוּ	אֵין עוֹד	וּשְׁכִינַת
our King is true	there is nothing else	Hashem's Presence

V'AL KEIN

The day will come when the whole world
will recognize and accept Hashem as King.

1 וְעַל כֵּן, נְקַוֶּה לְךָ, יְיָ אֱלֹהֵינוּ,
v'al *kayn* *n'ka·veh* *l'chuh* *Adonuy* *Elohaynu*

2 לִרְאוֹת מְהֵרָה בְּתִפְאֶרֶת עֻזֶּךָ.
leer·ohs *m'hay·ruh* *b'seef·eh·res* *u·zeh·chuh*

3 לְהַעֲבִיר גִּלּוּלִים מִן הָאָרֶץ,
l'ha·ah·veer *gi·lu·leem* *meen* *huh·uh·retz*

4 וְהָאֱלִילִים כָּרוֹת יִכָּרֵתוּן.
v'huh·eh·li·leem *kuh·ros* *yi·kuh·ray·soon*

5 לְתַקֵּן עוֹלָם בְּמַלְכוּת שַׁדַּי,
l'sa·kayn *o·lum* *b'mal·choos* *Shadai*

6 וְכָל בְּנֵי בָשָׂר יִקְרְאוּ בִשְׁמֶךָ,
v'chuhl *b'nay* *vuh·suhr* *yeek·r'u* *veesh·meh·chuh*

7 לְהַפְנוֹת אֵלֶיךָ, כָּל רִשְׁעֵי אָרֶץ,
l'haf·nos *ay·le·chuh* *kuhl* *reesh·ay* *uh·retz*

8 יַכִּירוּ וְיֵדְעוּ כָּל יוֹשְׁבֵי תֵבֵל,
ya·ki·ru *v'yay·d'u* *kuhl* *yo·sh'vay* *say·vayl*

9 כִּי לְךָ תִּכְרַע כָּל בֶּרֶךְ, תִּשָּׁבַע כָּל לָשׁוֹן.
ki *l'chuh* *teech·ra* *kuhl* *beh·rech* *ti·shuh·va* *kuhl* *luh·shon*

נְקַוֶּה	לְתַקֵּן עוֹלָם	יִקְרְאוּ בִשְׁמֶךָ	יַכִּירוּ
we hope	to perfect the world	they will call Your Name	they will recognize

l'fuh·ne·chuh | Adonuy | Elohaynu | yeech·r'u | v'yi·po·lu
1 | לְפָנֶיךָ יְיָ אֱלֹהֵינוּ, יִכְרְעוּ וְיִפֹּלוּ,

v'leech·vod | Sheem·chuh | y'kuhr | yi·tay·nu
2 | וְלִכְבוֹד שִׁמְךָ יְקָר יִתֵּנוּ,

vi·kab'lu | chu·lum | ah·lay·hem | es | ol | mal·chu·seh·chuh
3 | וִיקַבְּלוּ כֻלָּם עֲלֵיהֶם אֶת עוֹל מַלְכוּתֶךָ,

v'seem·loch | a·lay·hem | m'hay·ruh | l'o·lum | vuh·ed
4 | וְתִמְלֹךְ עֲלֵיהֶם מְהֵרָה לְעֹלָם וָעֶד,

ki | ha·mal·choos | sheh·l'chuh | hee
5 | כִּי הַמַּלְכוּת שֶׁלְּךָ הִיא,

ool·o·l'may | ahd | teem·loch | b'chuh·vod
6 | וּלְעוֹלְמֵי עַד תִּמְלֹךְ בְּכָבוֹד.

ka·kuh·soov | b'So·ruh·seh·chuh | Adonuy | yeem·loch | l'o·lum | vuh·ed
7 | כַּכָּתוּב בְּתוֹרָתֶךָ: יְיָ יִמְלֹךְ לְעֹלָם וָעֶד.

v'ne·eh·mar | v'huh·yuh | Adonuy | l'Meh·lech | al | kuhl | huh·uh·retz
8 | וְנֶאֱמַר: וְהָיָה יְיָ לְמֶלֶךְ עַל כָּל הָאָרֶץ,

ba·yohm | ha·hu | yeeh·yeh | Adonuy | Eh·chud | oosh·mo | Eh·chud
9 | בַּיּוֹם הַהוּא יִהְיֶה יְיָ אֶחָד, וּשְׁמוֹ אֶחָד.

When praying with a *minyan*, mourners recite *Kaddish Yosom* (page 76).

וִיקַבְּלוּ	עוֹל	תִּמְלֹךְ	אֶחָד
they will accept	responsibility	You will rule	one

AL TIRA Do not fear anything, for Hashem is always with us.

1 אַל תִּירָא מִפַּחַד פִּתְאֹם,
   al ti·ruh mi·pa·chad pees·ohm

2 וּמִשֹּׁאַת רְשָׁעִים כִּי תָבֹא.
   u·mi·sho·ahs r'shuh·eem ki suh·vo

3 עֻצוּ עֵצָה וְתֻפָר,
   u·tzu ay·tzuh v'su·fuhr

4 דַּבְּרוּ דָבָר וְלֹא יָקוּם,
   da·b'ru duh·vuhr v'lo yuh·koom

5 כִּי עִמָּנוּ אֵל.
   ki ee·muh·nu Ayl

6 וְעַד זִקְנָה אֲנִי הוּא, וְעַד שֵׂיבָה אֲנִי אֶסְבֹּל,
   v'ahd zeek·nuh A·ni Hu v'ahd say·vuh A·ni es·bol

7 אֲנִי עָשִׂיתִי, וַאֲנִי אֶשָּׂא, וַאֲנִי אֶסְבֹּל וַאֲמַלֵּט.
   A·ni uh·si·si va·A·ni eh·suh va·A·ni es·bol va·ah·ma·layt

8 אַךְ צַדִּיקִים יוֹדוּ לִשְׁמֶךָ,
   ach tza·dee·keem yo·du leesh·meh·chuh

9 יֵשְׁבוּ יְשָׁרִים אֶת פָּנֶיךָ.
   yay·sh'vu y'shuh·reem es puh·ne·chuh

When praying with a *minyan*, mourners study designated Mishnayos and recite *Kaddish Derabanan* (page 76).

אַל תִּירָא   עִמָּנוּ אֵ-ל
do not fear   Hashem is with us

SIX REMEMBRANCES   The Torah tells us to remember these six things every day.

1) Remember that Hashem redeemed us from Egypt.

meetz·ra·yeem · may·eh·retz · tzay·s'chuh · yohm · es · teez·kor · l'ma·ahn

לְמַעַן תִּזְכֹּר אֶת יוֹם צֵאתְךָ מֵאֶרֶץ מִצְרַיִם,

cha·yeh·chuh · y'may · kol

כֹּל יְמֵי חַיֶּיךָ.

2) Forget not when you stood at Mt. Sinai before Hashem.

b'cho·rayv · Elohechuh · Adonuy · leef·nay · uh·ma·d'tuh · ah·sher · yohm · teesh·kach · pen

פֶּן תִּשְׁכַּח... יוֹם אֲשֶׁר עָמַדְתָּ לִפְנֵי יְיָ אֱלֹהֶיךָ בְּחֹרֵב.

3) Remember Amalek's attempt to diminish your excitement for the Torah. Erase their memory.

a·muh·layk · zeh·cher · es · teem·cheh · a·muh·layk · l'chuh · uh·suh · ah·sher · ais · zuh·chor

זָכוֹר אֵת אֲשֶׁר עָשָׂה לְךָ עֲמָלֵק, ...תִּמְחֶה אֶת זֵכֶר עֲמָלֵק.

4) Remember how you upset Hashem in the desert.

teesh·kach · al · z'chor

זְכֹר אַל תִּשְׁכַּח,

ba·meed·buhr · Elohechuh · Adonuy · es · heek·tzaf·tuh · ah·sher · ais

אֵת אֲשֶׁר הִקְצַפְתָּ אֶת יְיָ אֱלֹהֶיךָ בַּמִּדְבָּר.

5) Remember how Miriam was punished for her Lashon Harah in the desert.

l'Meer·yum · Elohechuh · Adonuy · uh·suh · ah·sher · ais · zuh·chor

זָכוֹר אֵת אֲשֶׁר עָשָׂה יְיָ אֱלֹהֶיךָ לְמִרְיָם,

mi·meetz·ruh·yeem · b'tzay·s'chem · ba·deh·rech

בַּדֶּרֶךְ בְּצֵאתְכֶם מִמִּצְרָיִם.

6) Remember and observe the holy Shabbos day.

l'ka·d'sho · ha·Shabbos · yohm · es · zuh·chor

זָכוֹר אֶת יוֹם הַשַּׁבָּת לְקַדְּשׁוֹ.

KADDISH The Kaddish is praise to Hashem. It divides between sections of our Tefila and is said for some family members who passed away.

There are several versions of *Kaddish*. All begin with the "Half *Kaddish*" (this page), and then continue with their various inserts (next few pages), as applicable.

Kaddish is a responsive prayer. Listeners respond with "*Amein*" after each phrase.

1

yees·ga·dal	v'yees·ka·dahsh	Sh'mayh	ra·buh	"Amein"
יִתְגַּדַּל	וְיִתְקַדַּשׁ	שְׁמֵהּ	רַבָּא.	

2

b'uh·l'muh	dee	v'ruh	chir·oo·sayh	v'yahm·leech	mal·chu·sayh
בְּעָלְמָא	דִּי	בְרָא	כִרְעוּתֵהּ,	וְיַמְלִיךְ	מַלְכוּתֵהּ,

3

v'yatz·mach	poor·kuh·nayh	vi·kuh·rayv	m'shi·chayh	"Amein"
וְיַצְמַח	פּוּרְקָנֵהּ	וִיקָרֵב	מְשִׁיחֵהּ.	

4

b'cha·yay·chon	oov·yo·may·chon	oov·cha·yay	d'chuhl	bays	Yisroel
בְּחַיֵּיכוֹן	וּבְיוֹמֵיכוֹן	וּבְחַיֵּי	דְכָל	בֵּית	יִשְׂרָאֵל,

5

ba·ah·guh·luh	u·veez·mahn	kuh·reev	v'eem·ru	uh·mayn	"Amein"
בַּעֲגָלָא	וּבִזְמַן	קָרִיב	וְאִמְרוּ	אָמֵן.	

Listeners say the following line **with concentration**; the one saying *Kaddish* repeats it and continues.

6

y'hay	Sh'mayh	ra·buh	m'vuh·rach	l'uh·lahm	ool·uh·l'may	uhl·ma·yuh	yees·buh·raych
יְהֵא	שְׁמֵהּ	רַבָּא	מְבָרַךְ	לְעָלַם	וּלְעָלְמֵי	עָלְמַיָּא.	יִתְבָּרַךְ,

7

v'yeesh·ta·bach	v'yees·puh·ayr	v'yees·ro·mum	v'yees·na·say
וְיִשְׁתַּבַּח,	וְיִתְפָּאַר,	וְיִתְרוֹמַם,	וְיִתְנַשֵּׂא,

8

v'yees·ha·duhr	v'yees·ah·leh	v'yees·ha·lul	Sh'mayh	d'kood·shuh	b'reech	Hu	"Amein"
וְיִתְהַדָּר,	וְיִתְעַלֶּה,	וְיִתְהַלָּל,	שְׁמֵהּ	דְּקוּדְשָׁא	בְּרִיךְ	הוּא.	

9

l'ay·luh	meen	kuhl	beer·chuh·suh	v'shi·ruh·suh	toosh·b'chuh·suh	v'ne·che·muh·suh
לְעֵלָּא	מִן	כָּל	בִּרְכָתָא	וְשִׁירָתָא	תֻּשְׁבְּחָתָא	וְנֶחֱמָתָא,

10

da·ah·mi·run	b'uh·l'muh	v'eem·ru	uh·mayn	"Amein"
דַּאֲמִירָן	בְּעָלְמָא,	וְאִמְרוּ	אָמֵן.	

> יְהֵא שְׁמֵהּ רַבָּא מְבָרַךְ לְעָלַם
> May Hashem's Great Name be Blessed forever

KADDISH D'RABONON – THE RABBIS' KADDISH INSERT

A mourner (and/or *Chazzan*) says this paragraph only at the start and end of the *tefila*.

1   עַל יִשְׂרָאֵל וְעַל רַבָּנָן.
ra·buh·nun   v'al   Yisroel   al

2   וְעַל תַּלְמִידֵיהוֹן, וְעַל כָּל תַּלְמִידֵי תַלְמִידֵיהוֹן.
sal·mi·day·hon   tal·mi·day   kuhl   v'al   tal·mi·day·hon   v'al

3   וְעַל כָּל מָאן דְּעָסְקִין בְּאוֹרַיְתָא,
b'o·ra·y'suh   d'uh·s'keen   mun   kuhl   v'al

4   דִּי בְאַתְרָא הָדֵין,
huh·dayn   v'ahs·ruh   dee

5   וְדִי בְכָל אֲתַר וַאֲתַר.
va·ah·sar   a·sar   v'chuhl   v'dee

6   יְהֵא לְהוֹן וּלְכוֹן שְׁלָמָא רַבָּא,
ra·buh   sh'luh·muh   ool·chon   l'hon   y'hay

7   חִנָּא וְחִסְדָּא וְרַחֲמִין,
v'ra·cha·meen   v'chees·duh   chee·nuh

8   וְחַיִּין אֲרִיכִין, וּמְזוֹנָא רְוִיחָא, וּפוּרְקָנָא,
u·foor·kuh·nuh   r'vi·chuh   oom·zo·nuh   a·ri·cheen   v'cha·yeen

9   מִן קֳדָם אֲבוּהוֹן דִּבִשְׁמַיָּא,
d'veesh·ma·yuh   A·vu·hon   kuh·dum   meen

10   וְאִמְרוּ אָמֵן:
uh·mayn   v'eem·ru
"Amein"

| רַבָּנָן | תַּלְמִידֵיהוֹן | וְרַחֲמִין |
| Rabbis | their students | mercy |

KADDISH TISKABEL INSERT

This paragraph is said only by the *Chazzan* during the *tefila*.

Yisroel	bays	d'chuhl	u·vuh·u·s'hon	tz'lo·s'hon	tees·ka·bayl	
יִשְׂרָאֵל	בֵּית	דְּכָל	וּבָעוּתְהוֹן	צְלוֹתְהוֹן	תִּתְקַבֵּל	1

	uh·mayn	v'eem·ru	veesh·ma·yuh	dee	a·vu·hon	kuh·dum	
"Amein"	אָמֵן.	וְאִמְרוּ	בִּשְׁמַיָּא,	דִּי	אֲבוּהוֹן	קֳדָם	2

Continue here for Kaddish d'Rabonon, Tiskabel and Yasom (Mourner's)

sh'ma·yuh	meen	ra·buh	sh'luh·muh	y'hay	
שְׁמַיָּא,	מִן	רַבָּא	שְׁלָמָא	יְהֵא	3

	uh·lay·nu	toh·veem	v'cha·yeem	
	עָלֵינוּ,	טוֹבִים	וְחַיִּים	4

	uh·mayn	v'eem·ru	Yisroel	kuhl	v'al	
"Amein"	אָמֵן.	וְאִמְרוּ	יִשְׂרָאֵל,	כָּל	וְעַל	5

Kaddish Sayer: Take three steps back. Bow to the right while saying עֹשֶׂה שָׁלוֹם בִּמְרוֹמָיו then forward while saying הוּא; to the left while saying יַעֲשֶׂה שָׁלוֹם עָלֵינוּ and forward again while saying וְעַל כָּל יִשְׂרָאֵל וְאִמְרוּ אָמֵן.

	beem·ro·muv	ha·shuh·lom	o·seh	
During the *Aseres Y'mei Teshuva* add "ha-הַ."	בִּמְרוֹמָיו,	הַשָּׁלוֹם	עֹשֶׂה	6

	uh·lay·nu	shuh·lom	ya·ah·seh	Hu	
	עָלֵינוּ,	שָׁלוֹם	יַעֲשֶׂה	הוּא	7

	uh·mayn	v'eem·ru	Yisroel	kuhl	v'al	
"Amein"	אָמֵן.	וְאִמְרוּ	יִשְׂרָאֵל,	כָּל	וְעַל	8

הוּא יַעֲשֶׂה שָׁלוֹם עָלֵינוּ	עֹשֶׂה שָׁלוֹם בִּמְרוֹמָיו
He shall make peace for us	He Who makes peace in the heavens

TRAVELER'S PRAYER — For a safe journey and return.

1. a·vo·say·nu vAylohay Elohaynu Adonuy mi·l'fuh·ne·chuh ruh·tzon y'hee
יְהִי רָצוֹן מִלְּפָנֶיךָ יְיָ אֱלֹהֵינוּ וֵאלֹהֵי אֲבוֹתֵינוּ,

2. l'shuh·lom v'satz·ee·day·nu l'shuh·lom sheh·toh·li·chay·nu
שֶׁתּוֹלִיכֵנוּ לְשָׁלוֹם, וְתַצְעִידֵנוּ לְשָׁלוֹם,

3. l'shuh·lom vsees·m'chay·nu l'shuh·lom v'sahd·ri·chay·nu
וְתַדְרִיכֵנוּ לְשָׁלוֹם, וְתִסְמְכֵנוּ לְשָׁלוֹם,

4. ool·shuh·lom ool·seem·chuh l'cha·yeem chef·tzay·nu leem·choz v'sa·gi·ay·nu
וְתַגִּיעֵנוּ לִמְחוֹז חֶפְצֵנוּ, לְחַיִּים וּלְשִׂמְחָה וּלְשָׁלוֹם,

5. If returning the same day: (l'shuh·lom v'sa·cha·zi·ray·nu)
(וְתַחֲזִירֵנוּ לְשָׁלוֹם),

6. ba·deh·rech ruh·ohs v'cha·yos v'lees·teem v'o·rayv o·yayv kuhl mi·kaf v'sa·tzi·lay·nu
וְתַצִּילֵנוּ מִכַּף כָּל אוֹיֵב וְאוֹרֵב וְלִסְטִים וְחַיּוֹת רָעוֹת בַּדֶּרֶךְ,

7. l'o·lum u·vuh·ohs ha·mees·ra·g'shos poor·uh·ni·yos u·mi·kuhl
וּמִכָּל פּוּרְעָנִיּוֹת הַמִּתְרַגְּשׁוֹת וּבָאוֹת לְעוֹלָם,

8. yuh·day·nu ma·ah·say b'chuhl b'ruh·chuh v'seesh·lach
וְתִשְׁלַח בְּרָכָה בְּכָל מַעֲשֵׂה יָדֵינוּ,

9. ool·ra·cha·meem ool·che·sed l'chayn v'si·t'nay·ni
וְתִתְּנֵנִי לְחֵן וּלְחֶסֶד וּלְרַחֲמִים,

10. to·veem cha·suh·deem v'seeg·m'laynu ro·ay·nu chuhl oov·ay·nay b'ay·ne·chuh
בְּעֵינֶיךָ וּבְעֵינֵי כָל רוֹאֵינוּ, וְתִגְמְלֵנוּ חֲסָדִים טוֹבִים,

11. peh kuhl t'fee·las sho·may·ah Ah·tuh ki t'fee·luh·say·nu kol v'seesh·ma
וְתִשְׁמַע קוֹל תְּפִלָּתֵנוּ, כִּי אַתָּה שׁוֹמֵעַ תְּפִלַּת כָּל פֶּה.

12. t'fee·luh sho·may·ah Adonuy Ah·tuh Bo·ruch
בָּרוּךְ אַתָּה יְיָ, שׁוֹמֵעַ תְּפִלָּה.

שֶׁתּוֹלִיכֵנוּ לְשָׁלוֹם — lead us in peace
וְתַדְרִיכֵנוּ לְשָׁלוֹם — guide us in peace
וְתַחֲזִירֵנוּ לְשָׁלוֹם — return us in peace

COMMON BRACHOS

Brachos for wondrous natural sights and sounds, and common Mitzvos.

Recite the beginning of the *bracha* and continue with its proper ending.

huh·o·lum   Meh·lech   Elohaynu   Adonuy   Ah·tuh   Bo·ruch

בָּרוּךְ אַתָּה יְיָ, אֱלֹהֵינוּ, מֶלֶךְ הָעוֹלָם... 1

When we see lightning, we say:

v'ray·shees   ma·ah·say   o·say

...עֹשֶׂה מַעֲשֵׂה בְרֵאשִׁית. 2

When we hear thunder, we say:

o·lum   muh·lay   oog·vu·ruh·so   sheh·ko·cho

...שֶׁכֹּחוֹ וּגְבוּרָתוֹ מָלֵא עוֹלָם. 3

When we see a rainbow, we say:

b'ma·ah·muh·ro   v'ka·yum   beev·ri·so   v'neh·eh·mun   ha·b'rees   zo·chayr

...זוֹכֵר הַבְּרִית, וְנֶאֱמָן בִּבְרִיתוֹ, וְקַיָּם בְּמַאֲמָרוֹ. 4

For these *brachos*, after בָּרוּךְ אַתָּה...הָעוֹלָם add this:

v'tzi·vuh·nu   b'meetz·vo·suv   ki·d'shuh·nu   ah·sher

אֲשֶׁר קִדְּשָׁנוּ בְּמִצְוֹתָיו, וְצִוָּנוּ... 5

When affixing a *mezuzah* on our doors, we say:

mezuzah   leek·bo·ah

לִקְבּוֹעַ מְזוּזָה. 6

When separating *challah*, we say:

cha·luh   l'haf·reesh

לְהַפְרִישׁ חַלָּה. 7

When immersing dishes or utensils* in the *mikvah*, we say:

kay·leem   *for one vessel* →   ke·li   t'vi·las   al

עַל טְבִילַת: כְּלִי ← *for multiple vessels*   כֵּלִים. 8

We immerse utensils used for food preparation, serving or eating that touch the food.

BEDTIME SHEMA

As we prepare for bed, we reflect on our conduct during the day and commit to a better tomorrow. We forgive anyone who may have wronged us, and ask Hashem to do the same for us.

For weekdays:

1   רִבּוֹנוֹ שֶׁל עוֹלָם,
ri·bo·no   shel   o·lum

2   הֲרֵינִי מוֹחֵל לְכָל מִי שֶׁהִכְעִיס וְהִקְנִיט אוֹתִי...
ha·ray·ni   mo·chayl   l'chuhl   mi   sheh·heech·ees   v'heek·neet   o·si

3   יְהִי רָצוֹן מִלְּפָנֶיךָ, יְיָ אֱלֹהַי, וֵאלֹהֵי אֲבוֹתַי,
y'hee   ruh·tzon   mi·l'fuh·ne·chuh   Adonuy   Elohai   vAylohay   a·vo·sai

4   שֶׁלֹּא אֶחֱטָא עוֹד...
sheh·lo   ech·tuh   ohd

5   וּמַה שֶּׁחָטָאתִי מְחוֹק בְּרַחֲמֶיךָ הָרַבִּים...
u·ma   sheh·chuh·tuh·si   m'chok   b'ra·cha·meh·chuh   huh·ra·beem

We now say the 3 paragraphs of *Shema, V'haya & Vayomer* (pages 40-45), and then continue below.

6   גָּד גְּדוּד יְגוּדֶנּוּ וְהוּא יָגֻד עָקֵב.
gud   g'dude   y'gu·deh·nu   v'hu   yuh·gude   uh·kayv

7   עָקֵב יָגֻד וְהוּא יְגוּדֶנּוּ גְּדוּד גָּד.
uh·kayv   yuh·gude   v'hu   y'gu·deh·nu   g'dude   gud

8   בְּיָדְךָ, אַפְקִיד רוּחִי, פָּדִיתָה אוֹתִי, יְיָ, אֵל אֱמֶת.
b'yuh·d'chuh   af·keed   ru·chi   puh·dee·suh   o·si   Adonuy   Ayl   e·mes

In preparation for the morning,
place a cup of water in a bowl near your bed, to be used for washing *netilas yodayim*.
See page 4 for details and the *bracha*.

אַפְקִיד רוּחִי	בְּיָדְךָ
I entrust my soul	in Your Hand

HAMAPIL Our final prayer before we drift into peaceful sleep.

1
huh·o·lum · Meh·lech · Elohaynu · Adonuy · Ah·tuh · Bo·ruch

בָּרוּךְ אַתָּה יְיָ, אֱלֹהֵינוּ, מֶלֶךְ הָעוֹלָם,

2
af·ah·pai · al · oos·nu·muh · ay·nai · al · shay·nuh · chev·lay · ha·ma·peel

הַמַּפִּיל חֶבְלֵי שֵׁנָה עַל עֵינַי, וּתְנוּמָה עַל עַפְעַפָּי,

3
uh·yeen · bas · l'ee·shon · u·may·eer

וּמֵאִיר לְאִישׁוֹן בַּת עָיִן.

4
a·vo·sai · vAylohai · Elohai · Adonuy · mi·l'fuh·ne·chuh · ruh·tzon · vi·hee

וִיהִי רָצוֹן מִלְּפָנֶיךָ, יְיָ אֱלֹהַי, וֵאלֹהֵי אֲבוֹתַי,

5
ool·shuh·lom · to·veem · l'cha·yeem · v'sa·ah·mi·day·ni · l'shuh·lom · sheh·tash·ki·vay·ni

שֶׁתַּשְׁכִּיבֵנִי לְשָׁלוֹם, וְתַעֲמִידֵנִי לְחַיִּים טוֹבִים וּלְשָׁלוֹם.

6
ra·yo·nai · y'va·ha·lu·ni · v'al

וְאַל יְבַהֲלוּנִי רַעְיוֹנַי,

7
ruh·eem · v'heer·hu·reem · ruh·eem · va·cha·lo·mos

וַחֲלוֹמוֹת רָעִים, וְהִרְהוּרִים רָעִים,

8
l'fuh·ne·chuh · sh'lay·muh · mi·tuh·si · oos·hay

וּתְהֵא מִטָּתִי שְׁלֵמָה לְפָנֶיךָ,

9
ha·muh·ves · ee·shan · pen · ay·nai · v'huh·ayr

וְהָאֵר עֵינַי, פֶּן אִישַׁן הַמָּוֶת.

10
beech·vo·doh · ku·lo · l'o·lum · ha·may·eer · Adonuy · Ah·tuh · Bo·ruch

בָּרוּךְ אַתָּה יְיָ, הַמֵּאִיר לְעוֹלָם כֻּלּוֹ, בִּכְבוֹדוֹ.

וַחֲלוֹמוֹת רָעִים	וְאַל יְבַהֲלוּנִי רַעְיוֹנַי	וְתַעֲמִידֵנִי לְחַיִּים טוֹבִים	שֶׁתַּשְׁכִּיבֵנִי לְשָׁלוֹם
bad dreams	may my thoughts not disturb me	wake me to a good life	may I lie down peacefully

YA'ALE V'YAVO — On special and holy days we ask Hashem to remember us and rebuild His Holy Temple in Jerusalem, with Moshiach.

1 Elohaynu vAylohay avosaynu, ya·ah·leh, v'yuh·vo, v'ya·gi·ah, v'yay·ruh·eh,
אֱלֹהֵינוּ וֵאלֹהֵי אֲבוֹתֵינוּ, יַעֲלֶה, וְיָבֹא, וְיַגִּיעַ, וְיֵרָאֶה,

2 v'yay·ruh·tzeh, v'yi·shuh·ma, v'yi·puh·kayd, v'yi·zuh·chayr, zeech·ro·nay·nu, u·fee·k'doh·nay·nu,
וְיֵרָצֶה, וְיִשָּׁמַע, וְיִפָּקֵד, וְיִזָּכֵר, זִכְרוֹנֵנוּ וּפִקְדוֹנֵנוּ,

3 v'zeech·rohn avosaynu, v'zeech·rohn muh·shi·ach ben Duh·veed av·deh·chuh,
וְזִכְרוֹן אֲבוֹתֵינוּ, וְזִכְרוֹן מָשִׁיחַ בֶּן דָּוִד עַבְדֶּךָ,

4 v'zeech·rohn Y'ru·shuh·la·yeem eer kud·sheh·chuh,
וְזִכְרוֹן יְרוּשָׁלַיִם עִיר קָדְשֶׁךָ,

5 v'zeech·rohn kuhl a·m'chuh bays Yisroel l'fuh·ne·chuh, leef·lay·tuh l'toh·vuh,
וְזִכְרוֹן כָּל עַמְּךָ בֵּית יִשְׂרָאֵל, לְפָנֶיךָ, לִפְלֵיטָה לְטוֹבָה,

6 l'chayn ool·che·sed ool·ra·cha·meem ool·cha·yeem toh·veem ool·shuh·lom b'yohm:
לְחֵן וּלְחֶסֶד וּלְרַחֲמִים, וּלְחַיִּים טוֹבִים, וּלְשָׁלוֹם, בְּיוֹם:

	On *Rosh Chodesh*: rosh ha·cho·desh ha·ze	On *Sukkos*: chag ha·su·kos ha·ze	7
	רֹאשׁ הַחֹדֶשׁ הַזֶּה	חַג הַסֻּכּוֹת הַזֶּה	
On *Pesach*: chag ha·ma·tzos ha·ze	On *Shemini Atzeres*:* sh'mi·ni a·tzeh·res ha·chag ha·ze	8
חַג הַמַּצּוֹת הַזֶּה	שְׁמִינִי עֲצֶרֶת הַחַג הַזֶּה	
On *Shavuos*: chag ha·shuh·vu·ohs ha·ze	On *Rosh Hashana*: ha·zi·kuh·rohn ha·ze	9
חַג הַשָּׁבֻעוֹת הַזֶּה	הַזִּכָּרוֹן הַזֶּה	

* and Simchas Torah

On *Yom Tov* add: "b'yohm tov meek·ruh ko·desh ha·zeh - בְּיוֹם טוֹב מִקְרָא קֹדֶשׁ הַזֶּה"

10 zuch·ray·nu Adonuy Elohaynu bo l'toh·vuh, u·fok·day·nu vo leev·ruh·chuh,
זָכְרֵנוּ יְיָ אֱלֹהֵינוּ בּוֹ לְטוֹבָה, וּפָקְדֵנוּ בוֹ לִבְרָכָה,

11 v'ho·shi·ay·nu vo l'cha·yeem toh·veem.
וְהוֹשִׁיעֵנוּ בוֹ לְחַיִּים טוֹבִים.

12 u·veed·var y'shu·uh v'ra·cha·meem choos v'chuh·nay·nu, v'ra·chaym uh·lay·nu v'ho·shi·ay·nu,
וּבִדְבַר יְשׁוּעָה וְרַחֲמִים, חוּס וְחָנֵּנוּ, וְרַחֵם עָלֵינוּ וְהוֹשִׁיעֵנוּ,

13 ki ay·le·chuh ay·nay·nu, ki Ayl Meh·lech cha·noon v'ra·choom Uh·tuh.
כִּי אֵלֶיךָ עֵינֵינוּ, כִּי אֵל מֶלֶךְ חַנּוּן וְרַחוּם אָתָּה.

מָשִׁיחַ בֶּן דָּוִד — Moshiach (redeemer), the son of David

יְרוּשָׁלַיִם עִיר קָדְשֶׁךָ — Jerusalem, Your holy city

L'DOVID HASHEM ORI

We recite this Psalm from Rosh Chodesh Elul* through Hoshaana Rabba, as it refers to the High Holy Days and Sukkos.

* The first day of *Rosh Chodesh*

♫ 15

1 ee·ruh   mi·mi   v'yeesh·ee   O·ri   Adonuy   l'Duh·veed
לְדָוִד, יְיָ אוֹרִי וְיִשְׁעִי מִמִּי אִירָא,

2 ef·chud   mi·mi   cha·yai   muh·ohz   Adonuy
יְיָ מָעוֹז חַיַּי מִמִּי אֶפְחָד...

3 a·va·kaysh   o·suh   Adonuy   may·ais   shuh·al·ti   a·chas
אַחַת שָׁאַלְתִּי מֵאֵת יְיָ, אוֹתָהּ אֲבַקֵּשׁ,

4 cha·yai   y'may   kuhl   Adonuy   b'vays   sheev·ti
שִׁבְתִּי בְּבֵית יְיָ כָּל יְמֵי חַיַּי,

5 b'hay·chuh·lo   ool·va·kayr   Adonuy   b'no·ahm   la·cha·zos
לַחֲזוֹת בְּנֹעַם יְיָ וּלְבַקֵּר בְּהֵיכָלוֹ.

6 ruh·uh   b'yohm   b'su·ko   yeetz·p'nay·ni   ki
כִּי יִצְפְּנֵנִי בְּסֻכּוֹ בְּיוֹם רָעָה,

7 y'ro·m'may·ni   b'tzur   uh·huh·lo   b'say·sehr   yas·ti·ray·ni
יַסְתִּרֵנִי בְּסֵתֶר אָהֳלוֹ, בְּצוּר יְרוֹמְמֵנִי...

8 va·ah·nay·ni   v'chuh·nay·ni   ek·ruh   ko·li   Adonuy   sh'ma
שְׁמַע יְיָ קוֹלִי אֶקְרָא, וְחָנֵּנִי וַעֲנֵנִי...

9 cha·yeem   b'eh·retz   Adonuy   b'tuv   leer·ohs   heh·eh·mahn·ti   lu·lay
לוּלֵא הֶאֱמַנְתִּי לִרְאוֹת בְּטוּב יְיָ בְּאֶרֶץ חַיִּים.

10 Adonuy   el   v'ka·vay   li·beh·chuh   v'ya·ah·maytz   cha·zak   Adonuy   el   ka·vay
קַוֵּה אֶל יְיָ, חֲזַק וְיַאֲמֵץ לִבֶּךָ, וְקַוֵּה אֶל יְיָ.

When praying with a *minyan*, mourners recite *Kaddish Yasom* (page 76).
Then continue with concluding prayers (pages 68-75).

לְבֶּךָ	וְיַאֲמֵץ	חֲזַק	קַוֵּה אֶל ה'	ה' אוֹרִי
your heart	courage	strengthen	trust in Hashem	Hashem is my Light

V'AL HANISIM

Praise and thanks to Hashem for the miracles
He performed for us on Chanukah and Purim.

This *tefila* is recited in the *Amida* and *Birkas Hamazon* on *Chanukah* and *Purim*.

♫ 40

1.
ha·g'vu·ros · v'al · ha·poor·kun · v'al · ha·ni·seem · v'al
וְעַל הַנִּסִים, וְעַל הַפֻּרְקָן, וְעַל הַגְּבוּרוֹת,

2.
ha·neef·luh·ohs · v'al · ha·t'shu·ohs · v'al
וְעַל הַתְּשׁוּעוֹת, וְעַל הַנִּפְלָאוֹת,

3.
ha·ze · bee·z'mahn · huh·haym · ba·yuh·meem · la·ah·vo·say·nu · sheh·uh·si·suh
שֶׁעָשִׂיתָ לַאֲבוֹתֵינוּ בַּיָּמִים הָהֵם, בִּזְּמַן הַזֶּה.

If you forgot to say *"V'Al Hanisim"* in *Bentching*, begin here after *"Mimarom."*

4.
la·a·vo·say·nu · sheh·uh·suh · k'mo · ni·seem · luh·nu · ya·a·se · Hu · huh·Ra·cha·mun
הָרַחֲמָן, הוּא יַעֲשֶׂה לָנוּ נִסִּים כְּמוֹ שֶׁעָשָׂה לַאֲבוֹתֵינוּ

5.
ha·ze · bee·z'mahn · huh·haym · ba·yuh·meem
Continue with *"Bimei,"* below.　בַּיָּמִים הָהֵם בִּזְּמַן הַזֶּה.

ON CHANUKAH:

♫ 41

6.
u·vuh·nuv · chash·mo·nuh·ee · guh·dol · ko·hayn · Yo·chuh·nun · ben · Ma·tees·yuh·hu · bee·may
בִּימֵי מַתִּתְיָהוּ בֶּן יוֹחָנָן כֹּהֵן גָּדוֹל, חַשְׁמוֹנַאִי וּבָנָיו,

7.
Yisroel · a·m'chuh · al · huh·r'shuh·uh · yuh·vun · mal·choos · k'sheh·uh·m'duh
כְּשֶׁעָמְדָה מַלְכוּת יָוָן הָרְשָׁעָה עַל עַמְּךָ יִשְׂרָאֵל

8.
r'tzo·ne·chuh · may·chu·kay · u·l'ha·ah·vi·rum · Torah·seh·chuh · l'hahsh·ki·chum
לְהַשְׁכִּיחָם תּוֹרָתֶךָ, וּלְהַעֲבִירָם מֵחֻקֵּי רְצוֹנֶךָ,

9.
tzuh·ruh·sum · b'ais · luh·hem · uh·ma·d'tuh · huh·ra·beem · b'ra·cha·meh·chuh · v'Ah·tuh
וְאַתָּה בְּרַחֲמֶיךָ הָרַבִּים, עָמַדְתָּ לָהֶם בְּעֵת צָרָתָם,

---

הַנִּסִים	הַנִּפְלָאוֹת	בַּיָּמִים הָהֵם בִּזְּמַן הַזֶּה
the miracles	the wonders	in those days, at this time

1
ni·k'muh·sum · es · nuh·kam·tuh · dee·num · es · dahn·tuh · ri·vum · es · rav·tuh
רַבְתָּ אֶת רִיבָם, דַּנְתָּ אֶת דִּינָם, נָקַמְתָּ אֶת נִקְמָתָם,

2
m'ah·teem · b'yad · v'ra·beem · cha·luh·sheem · b'yad · gi·bo·reem · muh·sar·tuh
מָסַרְתָּ גִבּוֹרִים בְּיַד חַלָּשִׁים, וְרַבִּים בְּיַד מְעַטִּים,

3
tza·dee·keem · b'yad · u·r'shuh·eem · t'ho·reem · b'yad · u·t'may·eem
וּטְמֵאִים בְּיַד טְהוֹרִים, וּרְשָׁעִים בְּיַד צַדִּיקִים,

4
So·ruh·seh·chuh · o·s'kay · b'yad · v'zay·deem
וְזֵדִים בְּיַד עוֹסְקֵי תוֹרָתֶךָ.

5
buh·o·luh·meh·chuh · v'kuh·dosh · guh·dol · shaym · uh·si·suh · u·l'chuh
וּלְךָ עָשִׂיתָ שֵׁם גָּדוֹל וְקָדוֹשׁ בְּעוֹלָמֶךָ,

6
ha·ze · k'ha·yohm · u·foor·kun · g'doh·luh · t'shu·uh · uh·si·suh · Yisroel · u·l'a·m'chuh
וּלְעַמְּךָ יִשְׂרָאֵל עָשִׂיתָ תְּשׁוּעָה גְדוֹלָה וּפֻרְקָן כְּהַיּוֹם הַזֶּה.

7
bay·se·chuh · li·d'veer · vuh·ne·chuh · buh·u · kach · v'a·char
וְאַחַר כֵּן בָּאוּ בָנֶיךָ לִדְבִיר בֵּיתֶךָ,

8
meek·duh·sheh·chuh · es · v'ti·ha·ru · hay·chuh·le·chuh · es · u·fee·nu
וּפִנּוּ אֶת הֵיכָלֶךָ, וְטִהֲרוּ אֶת מִקְדָּשֶׁךָ,

9
kud·sheh·chuh · b'cha·tz'ros · nay·ros · v'heed·li·ku
וְהִדְלִיקוּ נֵרוֹת בְּחַצְרוֹת קָדְשֶׁךָ,

10
ay·lu · Chanukah · y'may · sh'mo·nas · v'kuh·v'u
וְקָבְעוּ שְׁמוֹנַת יְמֵי חֲנֻכָּה אֵלּוּ,

11
ha·guh·dol · l'Sheem·chuh · u·l'ha·layl · l'ho·dos
לְהוֹדוֹת וּלְהַלֵּל לְשִׁמְךָ הַגָּדוֹל.

וּרְשָׁעִים בְּיַד צַדִּיקִים	וְהִדְלִיקוּ נֵרוֹת	לְהוֹדוֹת וּלְהַלֵּל	לְשִׁמְךָ הַגָּדוֹל
wicked in the hands of righteous	they lit candles	to thank and praise	Your Great Name

On Purim:

♫ 42

	ha·bee·ruh	b'Shu·shan	v'Esther	Mordechai	bee·may	

1 בִּימֵי מָרְדְּכַי וְאֶסְתֵּר בְּשׁוּשַׁן הַבִּירָה,

huh·ruh·shuh   huh·mun   a·lay·hem   k'sheh·uh·mahd

2 כְּשֶׁעָמַד עֲלֵיהֶם הָמָן הָרָשָׁע,

ha·y'hu·deem   kuhl   es   u·l'a·bayd   la·ha·rog   l'hahsh·meed   bee·kaysh

3 בִּקֵּשׁ לְהַשְׁמִיד לַהֲרוֹג וּלְאַבֵּד אֶת כָּל הַיְּהוּדִים,

eh·chud   b'yohm   v'nuh·sheem   taf   zuh·kayn   v'ahd   mi·na·ar

4 מִנַּעַר וְעַד זָקֵן, טַף וְנָשִׁים, בְּיוֹם אֶחָד,

uh·suhr   sh'naym   l'cho·desh   uh·suhr   bee·sh'lo·shuh

5 בִּשְׁלֹשָׁה עָשָׂר לְחֹדֶשׁ שְׁנֵים עָשָׂר,

luh·voz   u·sh'luh·lum   ah·duhr   cho·desh   hu

6 הוּא חֹדֶשׁ אֲדָר, וּשְׁלָלָם לָבוֹז.

ah·tzuh·so   es   hay·far·tuh   huh·ra·beem   b'ra·cha·meh·chuh   v'Ah·tuh

7 וְאַתָּה בְּרַחֲמֶיךָ הָרַבִּים הֵפַרְתָּ אֶת עֲצָתוֹ,

b'ro·sho   g'mu·lo   lo   va·ha·shay·vo·suh   ma·cha·shav·toh   es   v'keel·kal·tuh

8 וְקִלְקַלְתָּ אֶת מַחֲשַׁבְתּוֹ, וַהֲשֵׁבוֹתָ לוֹ גְּמוּלוֹ בְּרֹאשׁוֹ,

huh·aytz   al   buh·nuv   v'es   o·so   v'suh·lu

9 וְתָלוּ אוֹתוֹ וְאֶת בָּנָיו עַל הָעֵץ.

הֵפַרְתָּ אֶת עֲצָתוֹ	חֹדֶשׁ אֲדָר
You cancelled his plan	the month of *Adar*

SEFIRAS HA'OMER

From Pesach to Shavuos (Matan Torah) are 49 days of preparation. We count the Omer and improve our character.

Some laws of *Sefiras Ha'Omer*

1. We count *Sefiras Ha'Omer* from the 2nd night of *Pesach* until *Shavuos* for a total of 49 days.

2. Each night, after the stars come out, we count the number of the *next* calendar day, since the Jewish day begins at nightfall. So, for example:

When Sunday, the 16th of *Nissan* is the 1st day of the *Omer*, then on Saturday night – *before* Sunday – we count the 1st day of the *Omer*. On Sunday night – before Monday – we count the 2nd day of the *Omer*, etc.

3. If we forget to count at night we do so the next day, but without the *bracha*.

4. If we forgot to count both at night and the next day, then we continue counting on the remaining nights, but without the *bracha*.

We recite the *bracha* standing, having in mind the day's count of *sefirah* and the *mida* of that day (e.g. *chesed*). We then ask Hashem, in "*Harachaman*," to rebuild the *Beis Hamikdosh*.

huh·oh·lum Meh·lech Elohaynu Adonuy Ah·tuh Bo·ruch

בָּרוּךְ אַתָּה יְיָ, אֱלֹהֵינוּ, מֶלֶךְ הָעוֹלָם,   1

huh·o·mehr s'fee·ras al v'tzi·vuh·nu b'meetz·vo·suv ki·d'shuh·nu ah·sher

אֲשֶׁר קִדְּשָׁנוּ בְּמִצְוֹתָיו, וְצִוָּנוּ עַל סְפִירַת הָעוֹמֶר.   2

Week #1

16th of Nissan	Day
טז נִיסָן	#1

3

luh·o·mehr eh·chud yohm ha·yohm

הַיּוֹם יוֹם אֶחָד לָעוֹמֶר.   4

li·m'ko·muh ha·meek·dush bays a·vo·das luh·nu ya·cha·zeer hu huh·Ra·cha·mun

הָרַחֲמָן הוּא יַחֲזִיר לָנוּ עֲבוֹדַת בֵּית הַמִּקְדָּשׁ לִמְקוֹמָהּ,   5

seh·luh uh·mayn v'yuh·may·nu beem·hay·ruh

בִּמְהֵרָה בְיָמֵינוּ, אָמֵן סֶלָה.   6

*הָרַחֲמָן...
che·sed sheh·b'che·sed
חֶסֶד שֶׁבְּחֶסֶד

יַחֲזִיר... עֲבוֹדַת בֵּית הַמִּקְדָּשׁ	בִּמְהֵרָה בְיָמֵינוּ	חֶסֶד
return the service of the *Beis Hamikdosh*	speedily in our days	kindness

Week #1

| | | 17th of Nissan | Day | 1 |
| | | יז נִיסָן | #2 | |

*הָרַחֲמָן...
g'vu·ruh sheh·b'che·sed
גְּבוּרָה שֶׁבְּחֶסֶד

luh·o·mehr yuh·meem sh'nay ha·yohm
הַיּוֹם שְׁנֵי יָמִים לָעוֹמֶר. — 2

| | | 18th of Nissan | Day | 3 |
| | | יח נִיסָן | #3 | |

*הָרַחֲמָן...
teef·eh·res sheh·b'che·sed
תִּפְאֶרֶת שֶׁבְּחֶסֶד

luh·o·mehr yuh·meem sh'lo·shuh ha·yohm
הַיּוֹם שְׁלֹשָׁה יָמִים לָעוֹמֶר. — 4

| | | 19th of Nissan | Day | 5 |
| | | יט נִיסָן | #4 | |

*הָרַחֲמָן...
ne·tzach sheh·b'che·sed
נֶצַח שֶׁבְּחֶסֶד

luh·o·mehr yuh·meem ar·buh·uh ha·yohm
הַיּוֹם אַרְבָּעָה יָמִים לָעוֹמֶר. — 6

| | | 20th of Nissan | Day | 7 |
| | | כ נִיסָן | #5 | |

*הָרַחֲמָן...
hod sheh·b'che·sed
הוֹד שֶׁבְּחֶסֶד

luh·o·mehr yuh·meem cha·mi·shuh ha·yohm
הַיּוֹם חֲמִשָּׁה יָמִים לָעוֹמֶר. — 8

| | | 21st of Nissan | Day | 9 |
| | | כא נִיסָן | #6 | |

*הָרַחֲמָן...
y'sohd sheh·b'che·sed
יְסוֹד שֶׁבְּחֶסֶד

luh·o·mehr yuh·meem shi·shuh ha·yohm
הַיּוֹם שִׁשָּׁה יָמִים לָעוֹמֶר. — 10

yuh·meem sheev·uh ha·yohm
הַיּוֹם שִׁבְעָה יָמִים,

| | 22nd of Nissan | Day | 11 |
| | כב נִיסָן | #7 | |

*הָרַחֲמָן...
mal·choos sheh·b'che·sed
מַלְכוּת שֶׁבְּחֶסֶד

luh·o·mehr eh·chud shuh·vu·ah sheh·haym
שֶׁהֵם שָׁבוּעַ אֶחָד לָעוֹמֶר. — 12

מַלְכוּת	יְסוֹד	הוֹד	נֶצַח	תִּפְאֶרֶת	גְּבוּרָה	חֶסֶד
kingship	foundation	glory	victory	beauty	strength	kindness

*Return to page 88, line 5 for "...הָרַחֲמָן."

Week #2			

הָרַחֲמָן... *
che·sed sheh·beeg·vu·ruh
חֶסֶד שֶׁבִּגְבוּרָה

23rd of Nissan	Day #8	yuh·meem sh'mo·nuh ha·yohm	1
כג ניסן		הַיּוֹם שְׁמוֹנָה יָמִים,	

luh·o·mehr eh·chud v'yohm eh·chud shuh·vu·ah sheh·haym
שֶׁהֵם שָׁבוּעַ אֶחָד וְיוֹם אֶחָד לָעוֹמֶר. 2

הָרַחֲמָן... *
g'vu·ruh sheh·beeg·vu·ra
גְבוּרָה שֶׁבִּגְבוּרָה

24th of Nissan	Day #9	yuh·meem teesh·uh ha·yohm	3
כד ניסן		הַיּוֹם תִּשְׁעָה יָמִים,	

luh·o·mehr yuh·meem oosh·nay eh·chud shuh·vu·ah sheh·haym
שֶׁהֵם שָׁבוּעַ אֶחָד וּשְׁנֵי יָמִים לָעוֹמֶר. 4

הָרַחֲמָן... *
teef·eh·res sheh·beeg·vu·ruh
תִּפְאֶרֶת שֶׁבִּגְבוּרָה

25th of Nissan	Day #10	yuh·meem ah·suh·ruh ha·yohm	5
כה ניסן		הַיּוֹם עֲשָׂרָה יָמִים,	

luh·o·mehr yuh·meem oosh·lo·shuh eh·chud shuh·vu·ah sheh·haym
שֶׁהֵם שָׁבוּעַ אֶחָד וּשְׁלֹשָׁה יָמִים לָעוֹמֶר. 6

הָרַחֲמָן... *
ne·tzach sheh·beeg·vu·ruh
נֶצַח שֶׁבִּגְבוּרָה

26th of Nissan	Day #11	yohm uh·suhr ah·chad ha·yohm	7
כו ניסן		הַיּוֹם אַחַד עָשָׂר יוֹם,	

luh·o·mehr yuh·meem v'ar·buh·uh eh·chud shuh·vu·ah sheh·haym
שֶׁהֵם שָׁבוּעַ אֶחָד וְאַרְבָּעָה יָמִים לָעוֹמֶר. 8

הָרַחֲמָן... *
hod sheh·beeg·vu·ruh
הוֹד שֶׁבִּגְבוּרָה

27th of Nissan	Day #12	yohm uh·suhr sh'naym ha·yohm	9
כז ניסן		הַיּוֹם שְׁנַיִם עָשָׂר יוֹם,	

luh·o·mehr yuh·meem va·cha·mi·shuh eh·chud shuh·vu·ah sheh·haym
שֶׁהֵם שָׁבוּעַ אֶחָד וַחֲמִשָּׁה יָמִים לָעוֹמֶר. 10

הָרַחֲמָן... *
y'sohd sheh·beeg·vu·ruh
יְסוֹד שֶׁבִּגְבוּרָה

28th of Nissan	Day #13	yohm uh·suhr sh'lo·shuh ha·yohm	11
כח ניסן		הַיּוֹם שְׁלֹשָׁה עָשָׂר יוֹם,	

luh·o·mehr yuh·meem v'shi·shuh eh·chud shuh·vu·ah sheh·haym
שֶׁהֵם שָׁבוּעַ אֶחָד וְשִׁשָּׁה יָמִים לָעוֹמֶר. 12

הָרַחֲמָן... *
mal·choos sheh·beeg·vu·ruh
מַלְכוּת שֶׁבִּגְבוּרָה

29th of Nissan	Day #14	yohm uh·suhr ar·buh·uh ha·yohm	13
כט ניסן		הַיּוֹם אַרְבָּעָה עָשָׂר יוֹם,	

luh·o·mehr shuh·vu·ohs sh'nay sheh·haym
שֶׁהֵם שְׁנֵי שָׁבוּעוֹת לָעוֹמֶר. 14

מַלְכוּת	יְסוֹד	הוֹד	נֶצַח	תִּפְאֶרֶת	גְבוּרָה	חֶסֶד
kingship	foundation	glory	victory	beauty	strength	kindness

*Return to page 88, line 5 for "...**הָרַחֲמָן**."

	Week #3	

הָרַחֲמָן...* che·sed sheh·b'teef·eh·res חֶסֶד שֶׁבְּתִפְאֶרֶת	yohm cha·mi·shuh ha·yohm הַיּוֹם חֲמִשָּׁה עָשָׂר יוֹם,	30th of Nissan Day ל נִיסָן #15	1
	luh·o·mehr eh·chud v'yohm shuh·vu·ohs sh'nay sheh·haym שֶׁהֵם שְׁנֵי שָׁבוּעוֹת וְיוֹם אֶחָד לָעוֹמֶר.		2
הָרַחֲמָן...* g'vu·ruh sheh·b'teef·eh·res גְּבוּרָה שֶׁבְּתִפְאֶרֶת	yohm shi·shuh ha·yohm הַיּוֹם שִׁשָּׁה עָשָׂר יוֹם,	1st of Iyar Day א אִיָּר #16	3
	luh·o·mehr yuh·meem oosh·nay shuh·vu·ohs sh'nay sheh·haym שֶׁהֵם שְׁנֵי שָׁבוּעוֹת וּשְׁנֵי יָמִים לָעוֹמֶר.		4
הָרַחֲמָן...* teef·eh·res sheh·b'teef·eh·res תִּפְאֶרֶת שֶׁבְּתִפְאֶרֶת	yohm sheev·uh ha·yohm הַיּוֹם שִׁבְעָה עָשָׂר יוֹם,	2nd of Iyar Day ב אִיָּר #17	5
	luh·o·mehr yuh·meem oosh·lo·shuh shuh·vu·ohs sh'nay sheh·haym שֶׁהֵם שְׁנֵי שָׁבוּעוֹת וּשְׁלֹשָׁה יָמִים לָעוֹמֶר.		6
הָרַחֲמָן...* ne·tzach sheh·b'teef·eh·res נֶצַח שֶׁבְּתִפְאֶרֶת	yohm sh'mo·nuh ha·yohm הַיּוֹם שְׁמוֹנָה עָשָׂר יוֹם,	3rd of Iyar Day ג אִיָּר #18	7
	luh·o·mehr yuh·meem v'ar·buh·uh shuh·vu·ohs sh'nay sheh·haym שֶׁהֵם שְׁנֵי שָׁבוּעוֹת וְאַרְבָּעָה יָמִים לָעוֹמֶר.		8
הָרַחֲמָן...* hod sheh·b'teef·eh·res הוֹד שֶׁבְּתִפְאֶרֶת	yohm teesh·uh ha·yohm הַיּוֹם תִּשְׁעָה עָשָׂר יוֹם,	4th of Iyar Day ד אִיָּר #19	9
	luh·o·mehr yuh·meem va·cha·mi·shuh shuh·vu·ohs sh'nay sheh·haym שֶׁהֵם שְׁנֵי שָׁבוּעוֹת וַחֲמִשָּׁה יָמִים לָעוֹמֶר.		10
הָרַחֲמָן...* y'sohd sheh·b'teef·eh·res יְסוֹד שֶׁבְּתִפְאֶרֶת	yohm es·reem ha·yohm הַיּוֹם עֶשְׂרִים יוֹם,	5th of Iyar Day ה אִיָּר #20	11
	luh·o·mehr yuh·meem v'shi·shuh shuh·vu·ohs sh'nay sheh·haym שֶׁהֵם שְׁנֵי שָׁבוּעוֹת וְשִׁשָּׁה יָמִים לָעוֹמֶר.		12
הָרַחֲמָן...* mal·choos sheh·b'teef·eh·res מַלְכוּת שֶׁבְּתִפְאֶרֶת	yohm v'es·reem eh·chud ha·yohm הַיּוֹם אֶחָד וְעֶשְׂרִים יוֹם,	6th of Iyar Day ו אִיָּר #21	13
	luh·o·mehr shuh·vu·ohs sh'lo·shuh sheh·haym שֶׁהֵם שְׁלֹשָׁה שָׁבוּעוֹת לָעוֹמֶר.		14

מַלְכוּת kingship	יְסוֹד foundation	הוֹד glory	נֶצַח victory	תִּפְאֶרֶת beauty	גְּבוּרָה strength	חֶסֶד kindness

*Return to page 88, line 5 for "...הָרַחֲמָן."

	Week #4	

Day #22 — 7th of Iyar (ז אייר)

הַיּוֹם שְׁנַיִם וְעֶשְׂרִים יוֹם,
yohm v'es·reem sh'na·yeem ha·yohm

שֶׁהֵם שְׁלֹשָׁה שָׁבוּעוֹת וְיוֹם אֶחָד לָעוֹמֶר.
luh·o·mehr eh·chud v'yohm shuh·vu·ohs sh'lo·shuh sheh·haym

הָרַחֲמָן...*
che·sed sheh·b'ne·tzach
חֶסֶד שֶׁבְּנֶצַח

Day #23 — 8th of Iyar (ח אייר)

הַיּוֹם שְׁלֹשָׁה וְעֶשְׂרִים יוֹם,
yohm v'es·reem sh'lo·shuh ha·yohm

שֶׁהֵם שְׁלֹשָׁה שָׁבוּעוֹת וּשְׁנֵי יָמִים לָעוֹמֶר.
luh·o·mehr yuh·meem oosh·nay shuh·vu·ohs sh'lo·shuh sheh·haym

הָרַחֲמָן...*
g'vu·ruh sheh·b'ne·tzach
גְבוּרָה שֶׁבְּנֶצַח

Day #24 — 9th of Iyar (ט אייר)

הַיּוֹם אַרְבָּעָה וְעֶשְׂרִים יוֹם,
yohm v'es·reem ar·buh·uh ha·yohm

שֶׁהֵם שְׁלֹשָׁה שָׁבוּעוֹת וּשְׁלֹשָׁה יָמִים לָעוֹמֶר.
luh·o·mehr yuh·meem oosh·lo·shuh shuh·vu·ohs sh'lo·shuh sheh·haym

הָרַחֲמָן...*
teef·eh·res sheh·b'ne·tzach
תִּפְאֶרֶת שֶׁבְּנֶצַח

Day #25 — 10th of Iyar (י אייר)

הַיּוֹם חֲמִשָּׁה וְעֶשְׂרִים יוֹם,
yohm v'es·reem cha·mi·shuh ha·yohm

שֶׁהֵם שְׁלֹשָׁה שָׁבוּעוֹת וְאַרְבָּעָה יָמִים לָעוֹמֶר.
luh·o·mehr yuh·meem v'ar·buh·uh shuh·vu·ohs sh'lo·shuh sheh·haym

הָרַחֲמָן...*
ne·tzach sheh·b'ne·tzach
נֶצַח שֶׁבְּנֶצַח

Day #26 — 11th of Iyar (יא אייר)

הַיּוֹם שִׁשָּׁה וְעֶשְׂרִים יוֹם,
yohm v'es·reem shi·shuh ha·yohm

שֶׁהֵם שְׁלֹשָׁה שָׁבוּעוֹת וַחֲמִשָּׁה יָמִים לָעוֹמֶר.
luh·o·mehr yuh·meem va·cha·mi·shuh shuh·vu·ohs sh'lo·shuh sheh·haym

הָרַחֲמָן...*
hod sheh·b'ne·tzach
הוֹד שֶׁבְּנֶצַח

Day #27 — 12th of Iyar (יב אייר)

הַיּוֹם שִׁבְעָה וְעֶשְׂרִים יוֹם,
yohm v'es·reem sheev·uh ha·yohm

שֶׁהֵם שְׁלֹשָׁה שָׁבוּעוֹת וְשִׁשָּׁה יָמִים לָעוֹמֶר.
luh·o·mehr yuh·meem v'shi·shuh shuh·vu·ohs sh'lo·shuh sheh·haym

הָרַחֲמָן...*
y'sohd sheh·b'ne·tzach
יְסוֹד שֶׁבְּנֶצַח

Day #28 — 13th of Iyar (יג אייר)

הַיּוֹם שְׁמוֹנָה וְעֶשְׂרִים יוֹם,
yohm v'es·reem sh'mo·nuh ha·yohm

שֶׁהֵם אַרְבָּעָה שָׁבוּעוֹת לָעוֹמֶר.
luh·o·mehr shuh·vu·ohs ar·buh·uh sheh·haym

הָרַחֲמָן...*
mal·choos sheh·b'ne·tzach
מַלְכוּת שֶׁבְּנֶצַח

מַלְכוּת	יְסוֹד	הוֹד	נֶצַח	תִּפְאֶרֶת	גְבוּרָה	חֶסֶד
kingship	foundation	glory	victory	beauty	strength	kindness

*Return to page 88, line 5 for "הָרַחֲמָן...".

Week #5

Day #29	14th of Iyar יד אִייר	Pesach Shayni פֶּסַח שֵׁנִי

ha·yohm teesh·uh v'es·reem yohm
הַיּוֹם תִּשְׁעָה וְעֶשְׂרִים יוֹם,

sheh·haym ar·buh·uh shuh·vu·ohs v'yohm eh·chud luh·o·mehr.
שֶׁהֵם אַרְבָּעָה שָׁבוּעוֹת וְיוֹם אֶחָד לָעוֹמֶר.

*הָרַחֲמָן...
che·sed sheh·b'hod
חֶסֶד שֶׁבְּהוֹד

Day #30	15th of Iyar טו אִייר

ha·yohm sh'lo·sheem yohm
הַיּוֹם שְׁלֹשִׁים יוֹם,

sheh·haym ar·buh·uh shuh·vu·ohs oosh·nay yuh·meem luh·o·mehr.
שֶׁהֵם אַרְבָּעָה שָׁבוּעוֹת וּשְׁנֵי יָמִים לָעוֹמֶר.

*הָרַחֲמָן...
g'vu·ruh sheh·b'hod
גְּבוּרָה שֶׁבְּהוֹד

Day #31	16th of Iyar טז אִייר

ha·yohm eh·chud u·sh'lo·sheem yohm
הַיּוֹם אֶחָד וּשְׁלֹשִׁים יוֹם,

sheh·haym ar·buh·uh shuh·vu·ohs oosh·lo·shuh yuh·meem luh·o·mehr.
שֶׁהֵם אַרְבָּעָה שָׁבוּעוֹת וּשְׁלֹשָׁה יָמִים לָעוֹמֶר.

*הָרַחֲמָן...
teef·eh·res sheh·b'hod
תִּפְאֶרֶת שֶׁבְּהוֹד

Day #32	17th of Iyar יז אִייר

ha·yohm sh'na·yeem u·sh'lo·sheem yohm
הַיּוֹם שְׁנַיִם וּשְׁלֹשִׁים יוֹם,

sheh·haym ar·buh·uh shuh·vu·ohs v'ar·buh·uh yuh·meem luh·o·mehr.
שֶׁהֵם אַרְבָּעָה שָׁבוּעוֹת וְאַרְבָּעָה יָמִים לָעוֹמֶר.

*הָרַחֲמָן...
ne·tzach sheh·b'hod
נֶצַח שֶׁבְּהוֹד

Day #33	18th of Iyar יח אִייר	Lag Ba'Omer ל"ג בָּעוֹמֶר

ha·yohm sh'lo·shuh u·sh'lo·sheem yohm
הַיּוֹם שְׁלֹשָׁה וּשְׁלֹשִׁים יוֹם,

sheh·haym ar·buh·uh shuh·vu·ohs va·cha·mi·shuh yuh·meem luh·o·mehr.
שֶׁהֵם אַרְבָּעָה שָׁבוּעוֹת וַחֲמִשָּׁה יָמִים לָעוֹמֶר.

*הָרַחֲמָן...
hod sheh·b'hod
הוֹד שֶׁבְּהוֹד

Day #34	19th of Iyar יט אִייר

ha·yohm ar·buh·uh u·sh'lo·sheem yohm
הַיּוֹם אַרְבָּעָה וּשְׁלֹשִׁים יוֹם,

sheh·haym ar·buh·uh shuh·vu·ohs v'shi·shuh yuh·meem luh·o·mehr.
שֶׁהֵם אַרְבָּעָה שָׁבוּעוֹת וְשִׁשָּׁה יָמִים לָעוֹמֶר.

*הָרַחֲמָן...
y'sohd sheh·b'hod
יְסוֹד שֶׁבְּהוֹד

Day #35	20th of Iyar כ אִייר

ha·yohm cha·mi·shuh u·sh'lo·sheem yohm
הַיּוֹם חֲמִשָּׁה וּשְׁלֹשִׁים יוֹם,

sheh·haym cha·mi·shuh shuh·vu·ohs luh·o·mehr.
שֶׁהֵם חֲמִשָּׁה שָׁבוּעוֹת לָעוֹמֶר.

*הָרַחֲמָן...
mal·choos sheh·b'hod
מַלְכוּת שֶׁבְּהוֹד

מַלְכוּת kingship	יְסוֹד foundation	הוֹד glory	נֶצַח victory	תִּפְאֶרֶת beauty	גְּבוּרָה strength	חֶסֶד kindness

*Return to page 88, line 5 for "הָרַחֲמָן..."

Week #6		

1 | הָרַחֲמָן...*
 che·sed sheh·bee·sohd
 חֶסֶד שֶׁבִּיסוֹד | yohm u·sh'lo·sheem shi·shuh ha·yohm
 הַיּוֹם שִׁשָּׁה וּשְׁלֹשִׁים יוֹם, | 21st of Iyar   Day
 כא אִיָּיר   #36

2 | | luh·o·mehr eh·chud v'yohm shuh·vu·ohs cha·mi·shuh sheh·haym
 שֶׁהֵם חֲמִשָּׁה שָׁבוּעוֹת וְיוֹם אֶחָד לָעוֹמֶר. |

3 | הָרַחֲמָן...*
 g'vu·ruh sheh·bee·sohd
 גְּבוּרָה שֶׁבִּיסוֹד | yohm u·sh'lo·sheem sheev·uh ha·yohm
 הַיּוֹם שִׁבְעָה וּשְׁלֹשִׁים יוֹם, | 22nd of Iyar   Day
 כב אִיָּיר   #37

4 | | luh·o·mehr yuh·meem oosh·nay shuh·vu·ohs cha·mi·shuh sheh·haym
 שֶׁהֵם חֲמִשָּׁה שָׁבוּעוֹת וּשְׁנֵי יָמִים לָעוֹמֶר. |

5 | הָרַחֲמָן...*
 teef·eh·res sheh·bee·sohd
 תִּפְאֶרֶת שֶׁבִּיסוֹד | yohm u·sh'lo·sheem sh'mo·nuh ha·yohm
 הַיּוֹם שְׁמוֹנָה וּשְׁלֹשִׁים יוֹם, | 23rd of Iyar   Day
 כג אִיָּיר   #38

6 | | luh·o·mehr yuh·meem oosh·lo·shuh shuh·vu·ohs cha·mi·shuh sheh·haym
 שֶׁהֵם חֲמִשָּׁה שָׁבוּעוֹת וּשְׁלֹשָׁה יָמִים לָעוֹמֶר. |

7 | הָרַחֲמָן...*
 ne·tzach sheh·bee·sohd
 נֶצַח שֶׁבִּיסוֹד | yohm u·sh'lo·sheem teesh·uh ha·yohm
 הַיּוֹם תִּשְׁעָה וּשְׁלֹשִׁים יוֹם, | 24th of Iyar   Day
 כד אִיָּיר   #39

8 | | luh·o·mehr yuh·meem v'ar·buh·uh shuh·vu·ohs cha·mi·shuh sheh·haym
 שֶׁהֵם חֲמִשָּׁה שָׁבוּעוֹת וְאַרְבָּעָה יָמִים לָעוֹמֶר. |

9 | הָרַחֲמָן...*
 hod sheh·bee·sohd
 הוֹד שֶׁבִּיסוֹד | yohm ar·buh·eem ha·yohm
 הַיּוֹם אַרְבָּעִים יוֹם, | 25th of Iyar   Day
 כה אִיָּיר   #40

10 | | luh·o·mehr yuh·meem va·cha·mi·shuh shuh·vu·ohs cha·mi·shuh sheh·haym
 שֶׁהֵם חֲמִשָּׁה שָׁבוּעוֹת וַחֲמִשָּׁה יָמִים לָעוֹמֶר. |

11 | הָרַחֲמָן...*
 y'sohd sheh·bee·sohd
 יְסוֹד שֶׁבִּיסוֹד | yohm v'ar·buh·eem eh·chud ha·yohm
 הַיּוֹם אֶחָד וְאַרְבָּעִים יוֹם, | 26th of Iyar   Day
 כו אִיָּיר   #41

12 | | luh·o·mehr yuh·meem v'shi·shuh shuh·vu·ohs cha·mi·shuh sheh·haym
 שֶׁהֵם חֲמִשָּׁה שָׁבוּעוֹת וְשִׁשָּׁה יָמִים לָעוֹמֶר. |

13 | הָרַחֲמָן...*
 mal·choos sheh·bee·sohd
 מַלְכוּת שֶׁבִּיסוֹד | yohm v'ar·buh·eem sh'na·yeem ha·yohm
 הַיּוֹם שְׁנַיִם וְאַרְבָּעִים יוֹם, | 27th of Iyar   Day
 כז אִיָּיר   #42

14 | | luh·o·mehr shuh·vu·ohs shi·shuh sheh·haym
 שֶׁהֵם שִׁשָּׁה שָׁבוּעוֹת לָעוֹמֶר. |

מַלְכוּת kingship	יְסוֹד foundation	הוֹד glory	נֶצַח victory	תִּפְאֶרֶת beauty	גְּבוּרָה strength	חֶסֶד kindness

*Return to page 88, line 5 for "...הָרַחֲמָן."

Week #7

הָרַחֲמָן...* che·sed sheh·b'mal·choos חֶסֶד שֶׁבְּמַלְכוּת	yohm v'ar·buh·eem sh'lo·shuh ha·yohm הַיּוֹם שְׁלֹשָׁה וְאַרְבָּעִים יוֹם, luh·o·mehr eh·chud v'yohm shuh·vu·ohs shi·shuh sheh·haym שֶׁהֵם שִׁשָּׁה שָׁבוּעוֹת וְיוֹם אֶחָד לָעוֹמֶר.	28th of Iyar כח אִיָּר	Day #43
הָרַחֲמָן...* g'vu·ruh sheh·b'mal·choos גְּבוּרָה שֶׁבְּמַלְכוּת	yohm v'ar·buh·eem ar·buh·uh ha·yohm הַיּוֹם אַרְבָּעָה וְאַרְבָּעִים יוֹם, luh·o·mehr yuh·meem oosh·nay shuh·vu·ohs shi·shuh sheh·haym שֶׁהֵם שִׁשָּׁה שָׁבוּעוֹת וּשְׁנֵי יָמִים לָעוֹמֶר.	29th of Iyar כט אִיָּר	Day #44
הָרַחֲמָן...* teef·eh·res sheh·b'mal·choos תִּפְאֶרֶת שֶׁבְּמַלְכוּת	yohm v'ar·buh·eem cha·mi·shuh ha·yohm הַיּוֹם חֲמִשָּׁה וְאַרְבָּעִים יוֹם, luh·o·mehr yuh·meem oosh·lo·shuh shuh·vu·ohs shi·shuh sheh·haym שֶׁהֵם שִׁשָּׁה שָׁבוּעוֹת וּשְׁלֹשָׁה יָמִים לָעוֹמֶר.	1st of Sivan א סִיָן	Day #45
הָרַחֲמָן...* ne·tzach sheh·b'mal·choos נֶצַח שֶׁבְּמַלְכוּת	yohm v'ar·buh·eem shi·shuh ha·yohm הַיּוֹם שִׁשָּׁה וְאַרְבָּעִים יוֹם, luh·o·mehr yuh·meem v'ar·buh·uh shuh·vu·ohs shi·shuh sheh·haym שֶׁהֵם שִׁשָּׁה שָׁבוּעוֹת וְאַרְבָּעָה יָמִים לָעוֹמֶר.	2nd of Sivan ב סִיָן	Day #46
הָרַחֲמָן...* hod sheh·b'mal·choos הוֹד שֶׁבְּמַלְכוּת	yohm v'ar·buh·eem sheev·uh ha·yohm הַיּוֹם שִׁבְעָה וְאַרְבָּעִים יוֹם, luh·o·mehr yuh·meem va·cha·mi·shuh shuh·vu·ohs shi·shuh sheh·haym שֶׁהֵם שִׁשָּׁה שָׁבוּעוֹת וַחֲמִשָּׁה יָמִים לָעוֹמֶר.	3rd of Sivan ג סִיָן	Day #47
הָרַחֲמָן...* y'sohd sheh·b'mal·choos יְסוֹד שֶׁבְּמַלְכוּת	yohm v'ar·buh·eem sh'mo·nuh ha·yohm הַיּוֹם שְׁמוֹנָה וְאַרְבָּעִים יוֹם, luh·o·mehr yuh·meem v'shi·shuh shuh·vu·ohs shi·shuh sheh·haym שֶׁהֵם שִׁשָּׁה שָׁבוּעוֹת וְשִׁשָּׁה יָמִים לָעוֹמֶר.	4th of Sivan ד סִיָן	Day #48
הָרַחֲמָן...* mal·choos sheh·b'mal·choos מַלְכוּת שֶׁבְּמַלְכוּת	yohm v'ar·buh·eem teesh·uh ha·yohm הַיּוֹם תִּשְׁעָה וְאַרְבָּעִים יוֹם, luh·o·mehr shuh·vu·ohs sheev·uh sheh·haym שֶׁהֵם שִׁבְעָה שָׁבוּעוֹת לָעוֹמֶר.	Erev Shavuos עֶרֶב שָׁבוּעוֹת 5th of Sivan ה סִיָן	Day #49

מַלְכוּת kingship	יְסוֹד foundation	הוֹד glory	נֶצַח victory	תִּפְאֶרֶת beauty	גְּבוּרָה strength	חֶסֶד kindness

*Return to page 88, line 5 for "הָרַחֲמָן...."

Here is your very own *Sefiras Ha'Omer* chart. Please copy this chart and post it in a noticeable place (fridge or desk etc.) and use it as your personal reminder for counting the *sefirah*!

If you can laminate it, you can use an erasable marker or cute stickers to mark off the dates you've already counted the *sefirah*.

Please ask your teacher or parent to make copies of the *sefirah* chart, and share them with your family and friends! This way, you are helping others do a *mitzvah*!

בס"ד

SEFIRAS HA'OMER CHART

NAME_____   FOR YEAR _____

| AND YOU SHALL COUNT FOR YOURSELVES FROM THE DAY AFTER THE HOLIDAY (PESACH)... SEVEN COMPLETE WEEKS THEY SHALL BE. | וּסְפַרְתֶּם לָכֶם מִמָּחֳרַת הַשַּׁבָּת... שֶׁבַע שַׁבָּתוֹת תְּמִימֹת תִּהְיֶינָה (וַיִּקְרָא כג: טו) |

EACH NIGHT, COUNT THE *SEFIRAH* FOR THE <u>NEXT</u> DAY.

WEEK #	S M W F	M T TH SH	S T W F	M W TH SH	S T TH F	M W F SH	S T TH SH
❶	1	2	3	4	5	6	7
❷	8	9	10	11	12	13	14
❸	15	16	17	18	19	20	21
❹	22	23	24	25	26	27	28
❺	29	30	31	32	33	34	35
❻	36	37	38	39	40	41	42
❼	43	44	45	46	47	48	49
🌹	ת	וֹ	ע	וֹ	ב	שַׁ	🌹

© Rabbi C.B. Alevsky, ToolsForTorah.com 5772/2012

Brachos for Food

with some Bentching

The rest of the Bentching and all related blessings are in the other editions of My Siddur

The music numbers 🎵02 are from Bentching Trax II.
This edition has just a few of the Bentching Trax, so the numbers skip around.

BRACHOS FOR FOOD   Blessings for food and drink.

Before we eat or drink anything – even the smallest bite or sip – we say a *bracha*.
This helps us be aware that our food – and everything else – comes from Hashem.

Each category of food has its very own special *bracha*. This is a very general list of the
foods and their *brachos*. For more details, check online for a list of food *brachos*.

For *Challah* and all kinds of bread, we first wash our hands using a large washing cup,
three times on the right and then three times on the left.

We raise our hands, rub them together and say:

huh·o·lum Meh·lech Elohaynu Adonuy Ah·tuh Bo·ruch

בָּרוּךְ אַתָּה יְיָ, אֱלֹהֵינוּ, מֶלֶךְ הָעוֹלָם,   1

yuh·duh·yeem n'ti·las al v'tzi·vuh·nu b'meetz·vo·suv ki·d'shuh·nu ah·sher

אֲשֶׁר קִדְּשָׁנוּ בְּמִצְוֹתָיו, וְצִוָּנוּ עַל נְטִילַת יָדָיִם.   2

We then dry our hands and say the *bracha* for the *Challah* or bread:

huh·o·lum Meh·lech Elohaynu Adonuy Ah·tuh Bo·ruch

בָּרוּךְ אַתָּה יְיָ, אֱלֹהֵינוּ, מֶלֶךְ הָעוֹלָם,   3

huh·uh·retz meen le·chem ha·mo·tzi

הַמּוֹצִיא לֶחֶם מִן הָאָרֶץ.   4

… for providing us with **bread**

Bread (or *Challah*) is considered the main/important food of a meal.
Wine (and grape juice) is considered the main/important drink of all drinks.
The *Hamotzi bracha* for bread includes all foods, and the *Hagafen bracha* for wine
includes all other drinks. Simply speaking: when eating a meal with bread, we do not
recite any food blessings, other than the initial *Hamotzi bracha,* during that meal.
Similarly, when drinking wine or grape juice, we do not bless over other drinks once
we have recited the *Hagafen bracha.*

For wine and grape juice:

ha·guh·fen   p'ri   bo·ray   huh·o·lum   Meh·lech   Elohaynu   Adonuy   Ah·tuh   Bo·ruch

בָּרוּךְ אַתָּה יְיָ, אֱלֹהֵינוּ, מֶלֶךְ הָעוֹלָם, בּוֹרֵא פְּרִי הַגָּפֶן.

… Who creates the **fruit of the grapevine**

For pastries, pasta, and other foods that contain flour:

m'zo·nos   mi·nay   bo·ray   huh·o·lum   Meh·lech   Elohaynu   Adonuy   Ah·tuh   Bo·ruch

בָּרוּךְ אַתָּה יְיָ, אֱלֹהֵינוּ, מֶלֶךְ הָעוֹלָם, בּוֹרֵא מִינֵי מְזוֹנוֹת.

… Who creates **all kinds of foods**/pastries

For the fruits of the tree (including nuts and berries, except for bananas):

huh·aytz   p'ri   bo·ray   huh·o·lum   Meh·lech   Elohaynu   Adonuy   Ah·tuh   Bo·ruch

בָּרוּךְ אַתָּה יְיָ, אֱלֹהֵינוּ, מֶלֶךְ הָעוֹלָם, בּוֹרֵא פְּרִי הָעֵץ.

… Who creates the **fruit of the tree**

For vegetables and all things that grow on the ground (including bananas):

huh·ah·duh·muh   p'ri   bo·ray   huh·o·lum   Meh·lech   Elohaynu   Adonuy   Ah·tuh   Bo·ruch

בָּרוּךְ אַתָּה יְיָ, אֱלֹהֵינוּ, מֶלֶךְ הָעוֹלָם, בּוֹרֵא פְּרִי הָאֲדָמָה.

… Who creates the **fruit of the earth**

For drinks, dairy, eggs, fish, meat, candy and just about everything else:

beed·vuh·ro   neeh·yuh   sheh·ha·kol   huh·o·lum   Meh·lech   Elohaynu   Adonuy   Ah·tuh   Bo·ruch

בָּרוּךְ אַתָּה יְיָ, אֱלֹהֵינוּ, מֶלֶךְ הָעוֹלָם, שֶׁהַכֹּל נִהְיָה בִּדְבָרוֹ.

… **everything** was created by His word

HAZON

Birkas Hamozon
After bread or Challah. (Only first paragraph here)

[20]

1. huh·o·lum Meh·lech Elohaynu Adonuy Ah·tuh Bo·ruch
בָּרוּךְ אַתָּה יְיָ, אֱלֹהֵינוּ, מֶלֶךְ הָעוֹלָם,

2. oov·ra·cha·meem b'che·sed b'chayn b'tu·vo ku·lo huh·o·lum es ha·zun
הַזָּן אֶת הָעוֹלָם כֻּלּוֹ בְּטוּבוֹ, בְּחֵן, בְּחֶסֶד, וּבְרַחֲמִים.

3. chas·doh l'o·lum ki buh·suhr l'chuhl le·chem no·sayn Hu
הוּא נוֹתֵן לֶחֶם לְכָל בָּשָׂר, כִּי לְעוֹלָם חַסְדּוֹ.

4. luh·nu chuh·sayr lo tuh·meed ee·muh·nu ha·guh·dol oov·tu·vo
וּבְטוּבוֹ הַגָּדוֹל עִמָּנוּ תָּמִיד, לֹא חָסֵר לָנוּ,

5. ha·guh·dol Sh'mo ba·ah·voor vuh·ed l'o·lum muh·zone luh·nu yech·sar v'al
וְאַל יֶחְסַר לָנוּ מָזוֹן לְעוֹלָם וָעֶד. בַּעֲבוּר שְׁמוֹ הַגָּדוֹל,

6. la·kol u·may·teev la·kol oom·far·nays zun Ayl Hu ki
כִּי הוּא אֵל זָן וּמְפַרְנֵס לַכֹּל, וּמֵטִיב לַכֹּל,

7. buh·ruh ah·sher b'ri·yo·suv l'chuhl muh·zone u·may·cheen
וּמֵכִין מָזוֹן לְכָל בְּרִיּוֹתָיו אֲשֶׁר בָּרָא,

8. ruh·tzon chai l'chuhl u·mas·bee·ah yuh·deh·chuh es po·say·ach kuh·uh·moor
כָּאָמוּר: פּוֹתֵחַ אֶת יָדֶךָ, וּמַשְׂבִּיעַ לְכָל חַי רָצוֹן.

9. ha·kol es ha·zun Adonuy Ah·tuh Bo·ruch
בָּרוּךְ אַתָּה יְיָ, הַזָּן אֶת הַכֹּל.

לְכָל בְּרִיּוֹתָיו | וּמֵכִין מָזוֹן | לֶחֶם | בְּחֵן בְּחֶסֶד וּבְרַחֲמִים | בְּטוּבוֹ | הַזָּן אֶת הָעוֹלָם כֻּלּוֹ
for all creatures | He prepares food | bread | grace, kindness and mercy | goodness | feeds the whole world

AL HAMICHYA	May·ayn Shalosh / Al Hamichya After certain grains, fruits, wine and grape juice.

huh·o·lum   Meh·lech   Elohaynu   Adonuy   Ah·tuh   Bo·ruch

בָּרוּךְ אַתָּה יְיָ, אֱלֹהֵינוּ, מֶלֶךְ הָעוֹלָם,   1

♫ 37

TYPE OF FOOD				START WITH	
THE FIVE GRAINS	ha·kal·kuh·luh הַכַּלְכָּלָה	v'al וְעַל	ha·meech·yuh הַמִּחְיָה	al עַל	2
WINE OR GRAPE JUICE	ha·ge·fen הַגֶּפֶן	p'ri פְּרִי	v'al וְעַל	ha·ge·fen הַגֶּפֶן	al עַל 3
THE FRUITS OF ISRAEL	huh·aytz הָעֵץ	p'ri פְּרִי	v'al וְעַל	huh·aytz הָעֵץ	al עַל 4

ha·suh·deh   t'nu·vas   v'al

וְעַל תְּנוּבַת הַשָּׂדֶה,   5

oor·chuh·vuh   toh·vuh   chem·duh   eh·retz   v'al

וְעַל אֶרֶץ חֶמְדָּה טוֹבָה וּרְחָבָה,   6

la·ah·vo·say·nu   v'heen·chal·tuh   sheh·ruh·tzi·suh

שֶׁרָצִיתָ וְהִנְחַלְתָּ לַאֲבוֹתֵינוּ,   7

mi·tu·vuh   v'lees·bo·ah   mi·peer·yuh   le·eh·chol

לֶאֱכֹל מִפִּרְיָהּ וְלִשְׂבּוֹעַ מִטּוּבָהּ.   8

פְּרִי הַגֶּפֶן fruit of the vine	פְּרִי הָעֵץ fruit of the tree	הַמִּחְיָה sustenance

1.   Elohaynu   Adonuy   nuh   ra·chem
רַחֵם נָא, יְיָ אֱלֹהֵינוּ,

2.   ee·reh·chuh   Y'ru·shuh·la·yeem   v'al   a·meh·chuh   Yisroel   al
עַל יִשְׂרָאֵל עַמֶּךָ, וְעַל יְרוּשָׁלַיִם עִירֶךָ,

3. hay·chuh·le·chuh   v'al   meez·b'che·chuh   v'al   k'vo·deh·chuh   meesh·kan   tzi·yohn   v'al
וְעַל צִיּוֹן מִשְׁכַּן כְּבוֹדֶךָ, וְעַל מִזְבְּחֶךָ, וְעַל הֵיכָלֶךָ.

4.   v'yuh·may·nu   beem·hay·ruh   ha·ko·desh   eer   Y'ru·shuh·la·yeem   oov·nay
וּבְנֵה יְרוּשָׁלַיִם עִיר הַקֹּדֶשׁ בִּמְהֵרָה בְיָמֵינוּ,

5.   vuh   v'sa·m'chay·nu   l'so·chuh   v'ha·ah·lay·nu
וְהַעֲלֵנוּ לְתוֹכָהּ, וְשַׂמְּחֵנוּ בָהּ,

6.   oov·tuh·huh·ruh   beek·du·shuh   oon·vuh·reh·ch'chuh
וּנְבָרֶכְךָ בִּקְדֻשָּׁה וּבְטָהֳרָה.

7.   ha·ze   ha·Shabbos   b'yohm   v'ha·cha·li·tzay·nu   oor·tzay   On *Shabbos* add:
וּרְצֵה וְהַחֲלִיצֵנוּ בְּיוֹם הַשַּׁבָּת הַזֶּה.

8.   ha·ze   ha·cho·desh   rosh   b'yohm   l'toh·vuh   v'zuch·ray·nu   On *Rosh Chodesh* add:
וְזָכְרֵנוּ לְטוֹבָה בְּיוֹם רֹאשׁ הַחֹדֶשׁ הַזֶּה.

9.   ha·ze   ha·zi·kuh·rohn   b'yohm   l'toh·vuh   v'zuch·ray·nu   On *Rosh Hashana* add:
וְזָכְרֵנוּ לְטוֹבָה בְּיוֹם הַזִּכָּרוֹן הַזֶּה.

10.   ha·ze   ha·ma·tzos   chag   b'yohm   l'toh·vuh   v'zuch·ray·nu   On *Pesach* add:
וְזָכְרֵנוּ לְטוֹבָה בְּיוֹם חַג הַמַּצּוֹת הַזֶּה.

11.   ha·ze   ha·shuh·vu·ohs   chag   b'yohm   l'toh·vuh   v'zuch·ray·nu   On *Shavuos* add:
וְזָכְרֵנוּ לְטוֹבָה בְּיוֹם חַג הַשָּׁבֻעוֹת הַזֶּה.

12.   ha·ze   ha·su·kos   chag   b'yohm   l'toh·vuh   v'zuch·ray·nu   On *Sukkos* add:
וְזָכְרֵנוּ לְטוֹבָה בְּיוֹם חַג הַסֻּכּוֹת הַזֶּה.

13.   ha·ze   ha·chag   ah·tzeh·res   sh'mi·ni   b'yohm   l'toh·vuh   v'zuch·ray·nu   On *Shemini Atzeres* and *Simchas Torah*:
וְזָכְרֵנוּ לְטוֹבָה בְּיוֹם שְׁמִינִי עֲצֶרֶת הֶחָג הַזֶּה.

וּנְבָרֶכְךָ
we will bless You

1   כִּי אַתָּה יְיָ טוֹב וּמֵטִיב לַכֹּל, וְנוֹדֶה לָךְ...

ki   Ah·tuh   Adonuy   tov   u·may·teev   la·kol   v'no·deh   l'chuh

---

FOR THE FIVE GRAINS

2   ...עַל הָאָרֶץ וְעַל הַמִּחְיָה.

al   huh·uh·retz   v'al   ha·meech·yuh

3   בָּרוּךְ אַתָּה יְיָ, עַל הָאָרֶץ וְעַל הַמִּחְיָה.

Bo·ruch   Ah·tuh   Adonuy   al   huh·uh·retz   v'al   ha·meech·yuh

---

FOR WINE OR GRAPE JUICE

4   ...עַל הָאָרֶץ וְעַל פְּרִי הַגָּפֶן.

al   huh·uh·retz   v'al   p'ri   ha·guh·fen

5   בָּרוּךְ אַתָּה יְיָ, עַל הָאָרֶץ וְעַל פְּרִי הַגָּפֶן.

Bo·ruch   Ah·tuh   Adonuy   al   huh·uh·retz   v'al   p'ri   ha·guh·fen

---

FOR THE SPECIAL FRUITS OF ISRAEL

6   ...עַל הָאָרֶץ וְעַל הַפֵּרוֹת.

al   huh·uh·retz   v'al   ha·pay·ros

7   בָּרוּךְ אַתָּה יְיָ, עַל הָאָרֶץ וְעַל הַפֵּרוֹת.

Bo·ruch   Ah·tuh   Adonuy   al   huh·uh·retz   v'al   ha·pay·ros

---

וְנוֹדֶה לָךְ	עַל הָאָרֶץ	הַמִּחְיָה	פְּרִי הַגֶּפֶן	הַפֵּרוֹת
we will thank You	for the land	sustenance	fruit of the vine	fruit of the tree

BOREI NEFASHOS   After all other food and drink.

Bo·ruch	Ah·tuh	Adonuy	Elohaynu	Meh·lech	huh·o·lum

בָּרוּךְ אַתָּה יְיָ, אֱלֹהֵינוּ, מֶלֶךְ הָעוֹלָם,   1

bo·ray	n'fuh·shos	ra·bos	v'ches·ro·nun

בּוֹרֵא נְפָשׁוֹת רַבּוֹת, וְחֶסְרוֹנָן,   2

al	kol	ma	sheh·buh·ruh·suh

עַל כֹּל מַה שֶׁבָּרָאתָ,   3

l'ha·cha·yos	buh·hem	ne·fesh	kuhl	chuy

לְהַחֲיוֹת בָּהֶם נֶפֶשׁ כָּל חָי,   4

Bo·ruch	chay	huh·o·luh·meem

בָּרוּךְ חֵי הָעוֹלָמִים.   5

בָּרוּךְ חֵי הָעוֹלָמִים
Blessed is the Life of the worlds

BRICH RACHAMANA   A short Birkas Hamozon for young children
to recite after eating bread.

B'reech	Ra·cha·muh·nuh	Eluhunuh	Mal·kuh	d'uhl·muh	muh·ruh	d'hai	pi·tuh

בְּרִיךְ רַחֲמָנָא, אֱלָהָנָא, מַלְכָּא דְעָלְמָא, מָרָא דְהַאי פִּיתָּא.   6

מָרָא דְהַאי פִּיתָּא	אֱלָהָנָא	רַחֲמָנָא	בְּרִיךְ
Master of this bread	our G-d	the Merciful One	Blessed is

THE 12 PESUKIM

12 PESUKIM   12 key ideas for every Jewish boy and girl
to live by, study and memorize.

1. THE TORAH IS REALLY MINE.

Moshe   luh·nu   tzi·vuh   Torah

תּוֹרָה צִוָּה לָנוּ מֹשֶׁה, 1

Ya·ah·kov   k'hee·las   mo·ruh·shuh

מוֹרָשָׁה קְהִלַּת יַעֲקֹב. 2

The Torah that Moshe commanded us is our inheritance.

2. HASHEM IS ONE, ALWAYS AND EVERYWHERE IN TIME, PLACE AND BEYOND.

Yisroel   sh'ma

שְׁמַע יִשְׂרָאֵל, 3

Eh·chud   Adonuy   Elohaynu   Adonuy

יְיָ אֱלֹהֵינוּ, יְיָ אֶחָד. 4

Hear O Israel, Hashem is our G-d, Hashem is One.

3. WE ARE ALWAYS ON THE JOURNEY TO A BETTER PLACE.

vuh·dor   dor   b'chuhl

בְּכָל דּוֹר וָדוֹר, ₁

atz·mo   es   leer·ohs   uh·dum   cha·yuv

חַיָּב אָדָם לִרְאוֹת אֶת עַצְמוֹ, ₂

mi·meetz·ruh·yeem   yuh·tzuh   hu   k'eelu

כְּאִלּוּ הוּא יָצָא מִמִּצְרָיִם. ₃

In every generation a person must consider him/herself
as if s/he personally left Egypt.

4. HASHEM IS PROUD OF US.

ha·buh   l'o·lum   chay·lek   luh·hem   yaysh   Yisroel   kuhl

כָּל יִשְׂרָאֵל, יֵשׁ לָהֶם חֵלֶק לְעוֹלָם הַבָּא, ₄

tza·dee·keem   ku·lum   v'a·maych   sheh·ne·eh·mar

שֶׁנֶּאֱמַר: וְעַמֵּךְ כֻּלָּם צַדִּיקִים, ₅

uh·retz   yi·r'shu   l'o·lum

לְעוֹלָם יִירְשׁוּ אָרֶץ, ₆

l'hees·puh·ayr   yuh·dai   ma·ah·say   ma·tuh·ai   nay·tzer

נֵצֶר מַטָּעַי, מַעֲשֵׂה יָדַי, לְהִתְפָּאֵר. ₇

Every Jew has a portion in the World to Come, as it says,
"And your nation are all righteous; they will inherit the land forever.
They are the branch of My planting, the creation of My hands, in which I take pride."

5. YES, WE CAN!

m'ohd · ha·duh·vuhr · ay·le·chuh · kuh·rov · ki

1 כִּי קָרוֹב אֵלֶיךָ הַדָּבָר מְאֹד,

la·ah·so·so · u·veel·vuh·v'chuh · b'fee·chuh

2 בְּפִיךָ וּבִלְבָבְךָ לַעֲשׂתוֹ.

For the thing (Torah & *mitzvos*) is very near to you (easy),
in your mouth (speech) and heart (feelings) to do it (action).

6. HASHEM KNOWS EVERYTHING... (AND WANTS YOU TO SUCCEED!)

uh·luv · ni·tzuv · Hashem · v'hee·nay

3 וְהִנֵּה ה' נִצָּב עָלָיו,

k'vo·doh · huh·uh·retz · chuhl · oom·lo

4 וּמְלֹא כָל הָאָרֶץ כְּבוֹדוֹ,

vuh·layv · k'luh·yos · u·vo·chayn · uh·luv · u·ma·beet

5 וּמַבִּיט עָלָיו, וּבוֹחֵן כְּלָיוֹת וָלֵב,

kuh·ruh·uy · o·v'doh · eem

6 אִם עוֹבְדוֹ כָּרָאוּי.

Hashem is standing over me; His glory fills the world. Hashem is looking at me,
examining my mind and heart, [verifying that] I am serving Him properly.

7. HASHEM CREATED EVERYTHING - FOR A PURPOSE.

♪ 88

Eloheem   buh·ruh   b'ray·shees

1   בְּרֵאשִׁית בָּרָא אֱלֹהִים,

huh·uh·retz   v'ais   ha·shuh·ma·yeem   ais

2   אֵת הַשָּׁמַיִם וְאֵת הָאָרֶץ.

In the beginning, Hashem created the heavens and the earth (everything).

8. LEARN AND TEACH TORAH: ALWAYS, EVERYWHERE.

♪ 89

bum   v'dee·bar·tuh   l'vuh·ne·chuh   v'shi·nan·tum

3   וְשִׁנַּנְתָּם לְבָנֶיךָ, וְדִבַּרְתָּ בָּם,

va·deh·rech   oov·lech·t'chuh   b'vay·seh·chuh   b'sheev·t'chuh

4   בְּשִׁבְתְּךָ בְּבֵיתֶךָ, וּבְלֶכְתְּךָ בַדֶּרֶךְ,

oov·ku·meh·chuh   oov·shuch·b'chuh

5   וּבְשָׁכְבְּךָ, וּבְקוּמֶךָ.

And you shall teach them (the words of Torah) to your children;
while at home and on the road, in the morning and in the evening.

9. REAL EFFORTS PRODUCE REAL RESULTS.

ta·ah·meen   al   muh·tzuh·si   v'lo   yuh·ga·ti

יָגַעְתִּי וְלֹא מָצָאתִי אַל תַּאֲמִין, 1

ta·ah·meen   al   u·muh·tzuh·si   yuh·ga·ti   lo

לֹא יָגַעְתִּי וּמָצָאתִי אַל תַּאֲמִין, 2

ta·ah·meen   u·muh·tzuh·si   yuh·ga·ti

יָגַעְתִּי וּמָצָאתִי תַּאֲמִין! 3

"I tried but did not succeed" - not true.
"I didn't (even) try but I succeeded" - not true.
"I tried and succeeded:" True!

10. LOVE YOUR FELLOW AS YOURSELF.

kuh·mo·chuh   l'ray·ah·chuh   v'uh·hav·tuh

וְאָהַבְתָּ לְרֵעֲךָ כָּמוֹךָ, 4

ba·Torah   guh·dol   k'lal   zeh   o·mayr   A·ki·vuh   ra·bee

רַבִּי עֲקִיבָא אוֹמֵר, זֶה כְּלָל גָּדוֹל בַּתּוֹרָה. 5

Love your fellow as yourself.
Rabbi Akiva says, "This is a great principle of the Torah."

11. MAKE HASHEM COMFORTABLE IN THIS WORLD: MAKE THIS WORLD A BETTER PLACE.

b'ri·uh·so   v'sach·lees   huh·uh·dum   kuhl   v'zeh

1 וְזֶה כָּל הָאָדָם, וְתַכְלִית בְּרִיאָתוֹ,

v'sach·toh·neem   el·yo·neem   huh·o·luh·mos   kuhl   oov·ri·ahs

2 וּבְרִיאַת כָּל הָעוֹלָמוֹת, עֶלְיוֹנִים וְתַחְתּוֹנִים,

b'sach·toh·neem   zu   dee·ruh   lo   leeh·yos

3 לִהְיוֹת לוֹ דִירָה זוֹ בְּתַחְתּוֹנִים.

The whole purpose of mankind and all of creation is for there to be a
dwelling place (home) for Hashem, in this lower (physical) world.

12. WE MAKE HASHEM HAPPY WHEN WE IMPROVE. SO LET'S REJOICE!

b'o·suv   Yisroel   yees·mach

4 יִשְׂמַח יִשְׂרָאֵל בְּעֹשָׂיו,

Yisroel   mi·zeh·ra   sheh·hu   mi   sheh·kuhl   pay·roosh

5 פֵּירוּשׁ, שֶׁכָּל מִי שֶׁהוּא מִזֶּרַע יִשְׂרָאֵל,

Hashem   b'seem·chas   lees·mo·ach   lo   yaysh

6 יֵשׁ לוֹ לִשְׂמוֹחַ בְּשִׂמְחַת ה',

b'sach·toh·neem   b'dee·ruh·so   v'suh·may·ach   sus   ah·sher

7 אֲשֶׁר שָׂשׂ וְשָׂמֵחַ, בְּדִירָתוֹ בְּתַחְתּוֹנִים.

"Israel should rejoice with its Creator (we should rejoice with Hashem)."
This means: Every Jew should rejoice in Hashem's joy,
as He rejoices in His home [here, on earth] below.

About the CD Trax Series

Many of the prayers overlap in all the various editions of My Siddur. Some of the Shabbat prayers are recited during the weekdays. Each edition of My Siddur has bits of "other" prayers, i.e. the "Weekday Edition" has a taste of Shabbat and Bentching, the "Weekday Holiday Edition" has a mini Shabbat section, etc. etc.

The CD - Audio Challenge

At this time, an audio CD holds just 70 minutes of audio. This created a real challenge for us to present all the audio of each section on one CD, in the order they appear in the Siddur. After much deliberation, this is what we came up with:

Each prayer section has its own CD.

Generally, each prayer is found on only one of the CDs, even though it is recited in multiple prayers. The Shabbat prayers that are also recited on weekdays, are found only on the weekday Tefila Trax and noted in the Shabbat sections with the unique, Tefila Trax music icon. (Therefore, the Shabbat Day Trax and music icons begin later in the Siddur (along with a few weekday prayers I could not fit into the weekday trax).

The musical icon in the Siddur notes the specific CD where that prayer is found.

1.   Weekday Prayers: Tefilah Trax
2.   Bentching and Shabbat Kiddush: Bentching Trax
3.   Friday Night Prayers: Kabalat Shabbat Trax
4.   Shabbat Day Prayers: Shabbat Day Trax
5.   Holiday Prayers: Holiday Trax

Also, due to the 70 minute limit on the audio CD, only the first line or few lines of many of the prayers have made it onto the CD.

MP3 Download in order of prayers

This CD time limit is limited to the CD... but not to MP3 downloads!

All the prayer tracks are also available for download in the order of the prayers in the Siddurim - in MP3 tracks. You can download the audio CD and MP3s on ToolsforTorah.com

See the complete list of CD trax and prayers in the following pages.

♫ 10

בְּרְכוֹת קְרִיאַת שְׁמַע וּשְׁמַע
Blessings of Shema & Shema

HaMa'riv Aravim	הַמַּעֲרִיב עֲרָבִים	34
Ahavat Olam	אַהֲבַת עוֹלָם	35
Shema	שְׁמַע	36
V'ahavta	וְאָהַבְתָּ	37-38
V'haya	וְהָיָה	39
Vayomer	וַיֹּאמֶר	40
Ve'emuna	וֶאֱמוּנָה	41
Mi Chamocha	מִי כָמֹכָה	42
Hashkivenu	הַשְׁכִּיבֵנוּ	43

עֲמִידָה: עַרְבִית לְלֵיל שַׁבָּת
Amida for Friday Night Arvit

#1 Magen Avraham	מָגֵן אַבְרָהָם	44
#2 Ata Gibor	אַתָּה גִבּוֹר	45
#3 Ata Kadosh	אַתָּה קָדוֹשׁ	46
Ata Kidashta	אַתָּה קִדַּשְׁתָּ	47
Vayechulu	וַיְכֻלּוּ	48
Yismechu	יִשְׂמְחוּ	49
#4 Elokeinu: R'tzay Na	אֱ-לֹקֵינוּ: רְצֵה נָא	50
#5 R'tzay	רְצֵה	51
#6 Modim	מוֹדִים	52
V'al Kulam	וְעַל כֻּלָּם	53
#7 Sim Shalom	שִׂים שָׁלוֹם	54
Yeeh'yu l'Ratzon	יִהְיוּ לְרָצוֹן	55
Elokai Netzor	אֱ-לֹקַי נְצוֹר	56
Oseh Shalom	עֹשֶׂה שָׁלוֹם	57

סוֹף תְּפִילַת עַרְבִית לְלֵיל שַׁבָּת
Concluding Friday Night Prayers

Vayechulu	וַיְכֻלּוּ	58
Chazzan's Bracha	בְּרְכַּת מֵעֵין שֶׁבַע	59
Magen Avot	מָגֵן אָבוֹת	60
Elokeinu: R'tzay Na	אֱ-לֹקֵינוּ: רְצֵה נָא	61
Hashem Ro·ee	מִזְמוֹר: ה' רֹעִי	62
Aleinu	עָלֵינוּ	63
V'al Kayn	וְעַל כֵּן	64-65
Al Tira	אַל תִּירָא	66

פֶּסַח Pesach

Burning the Chametz	עַל בְּעוּר חָמֵץ	43
Kol Chamira	כָּל חֲמִירָא	44
Kol Chamira	כָּל חֲמִירָא	45
Ma Nishtana	מַה נִּשְׁתַּנָּה	46
Sefirat Ha'Omer Blessing	סְפִירַת הָעֹמֶר	47
Counting the Omer	הַיּוֹם	48
Harachaman	הָרַחֲמָן	49
Tree Blessing	בִּרְכַּת הָאִילָנוֹת	50

🎵 **10**

Kabalat Shabbat Trax

Intro	01
Yedid Nefesh	יְדִיד נֶפֶשׁ	02
Shabbat Candle Lighting	נֵרוֹת שַׁבָּת	03

קַבָּלַת שַׁבָּת Welcoming Shabbat

L'chu Neranena	לְכוּ נְרַנְּנָה	04-05
Psalm 96	שִׁירוּ לַה'	06-07
Psalm 97	ה' מָלָךְ	08-09
Psalm 98	מִזְמוֹר שִׁירוּ	10-11
Psalm 99	ה' מָלָךְ	12-13
Mizmor L'David	מִזְמוֹר לְדָוִד	14-15
Ana B'Choach	אָנָּא בְכֹחַ	16
L'cha Dodi	לְכָה דוֹדִי	17-19
Shamor	שָׁמוֹר	20
Likrat	לִקְרַאת	21
Mikdash	מִקְדָּשׁ	22
Hitna'ari	הִתְנַעֲרִי	23
Hitoreri	הִתְעוֹרְרִי	24
Lo Tevoshi	לֹא תֵבוֹשִׁי	25
V'hayu	וְהָיוּ לִמְשִׁסָּה	26
Yamin	יָמִין	27
Bo'ee	בּוֹאִי	28
Shir L'yom HaShabbat	שִׁיר לְיוֹם הַשַּׁבָּת	29
Hashem Malach	ה' מָלָךְ	30
K'gavna	כְּגַוְנָא	31
Raza d'Shabbat	רָזָא דְשַׁבָּת	32
Barchu	בָּרְכוּ	33

Trax CDs Series

See more wonderful educational tools at:

www.ToolsforTorah.com

MW00450961

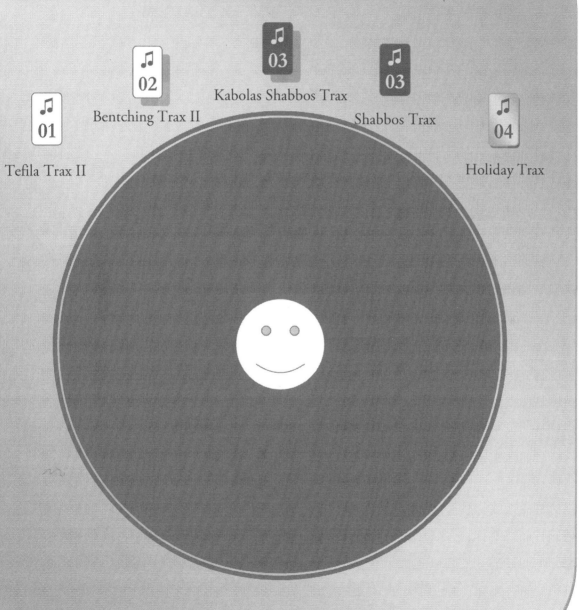

Tefila Trax II

Bentching Trax II

Kabolas Shabbos Trax

Shabbos Trax

Holiday Trax

If you have a CD please let it "rest" on Shabbat and the holy days.